Power and Equilibrium in the 1970s

Power and Equilibrium in the 1970s

Alastair Buchan

1973
CHATTO & WINDUS
LONDON

Published by
Chatto & Windus Ltd
42 William IV Street
London WC2N 4DF

ISBN 0 7011 1998 5

Printed in the United States of America

Contents

Preface

This brief analysis of the way in which the relationships between the major states and centres of power in the world appear to be changing, and of the new kinds of equilibrium which may emerge from this process of change, was originally prepared for an American audience. It was delivered as the Russell Leffingwell Lectures at the Council on Foreign Relations in New York (the sister institute of Chatham House) in April 1972, after President Nixon's visit to China in February but before his visit to Moscow in May of that year.

We are passing through a period of considerable change in the structure of international relations as the Soviet Union has achieved strategic parity with the United States, as a triangular political relationship has developed between Washington, Moscow and Peking, as Japan has emerged as the world's third strongest economic power, and as the European Community has become not only enlarged but has begun to create the framework of political as well as economic cohesion. The bipolar power structure of the post-war era which began to crumble in the early 1960s now seems to be disappearing, and there is much talk of "multipolarity" or of a new five-power balance.

Because of these developments, and because many Americans have viewed a multiple balance of power with scepticism or distrust, as characteristic of the manoeuvrings which drew first the European powers and then their own country into two world wars, I thought it useful to use the occasion of these lectures to discuss the whole notion of the balance of power. Are we really moving into a situation which bears any analogy with the operation of multiple great power balances of the past? If there is some validity to the idea, has the history of earlier multiple balances anything to teach us, or have developments such as nuclear weapons, mass communications, and democratic opinion permanently altered the way in which the great states interact? What is meant by that ambiguous metaphor "the balance of power"? What function have its classical protagonists seen it as performing? If the conception of a multiple balance in the 1970s and 1980s has some validity, how may we expect to see it operate?

I hope that some of the ideas which these essays contain may be of value to non-American readers, but I must emphasise that they are only a partial and preliminary analysis. For one thing, though they were written not very long ago, some references in them have already been overtaken by events: the agreements between the United States and the Soviet Union on arms control and technological and economic cooperation have proved more extensive than I assumed at the time I was writing: peace of a kind has been achieved in Vietnam: notably, the balance among the Western powers on the monetary and economic plane has proved even more unstable than I had assumed. This is, in any case, no moment for final judgements for we are in the midst of an "era of negotiations" on many fronts, arms control, east-west relations in Europe, monetary and trade negotiations, whose outcome may not be apparent for several more years. I hope, however, that the attempt to outline the different planes of power on which any analysis of balance in the modern world must rest may be useful in helping to interpret the swiftly unfolding pace of events.

I am grateful to Michael Howard for having read the manuscript in draft and for his comments, to several American friends for constructive criticism on a number of points, and to Mrs. Jessie Dougherty for her assistance in its preparation.

A.F.B.

Power and Equilibrium in the 1970s

I

A New Multiple
Balance of Power?

That we find ourselves in a different world in 1972 from that of 1962 or even 1968 needs no emphasis. If power in the contemporary world can be crudely divided into four instrumentalities—strategic power, tactical or conventional military strength, political influence, and economic strength —the distribution of these four forms of power among the major actors on the international scene is being transformed.

In the domain of strategic power—nuclear weapons and long-range means of delivery—the land-based forces of the

Soviet Union now exceed those of the United States in the ratio of 3 : 2 while her force of submarine-launched missiles is drawing level with that of the United States. In my view this may be one of the less significant changes that has occurred in the relationship of the major states, especially since the development of the MIRV (multiple independently targetable re-entry vehicle) has made quantitative calculations about relative strategic strengths even less relevant than before to the exercise of real political power. It is true, as President Nixon said at the beginning of 1972, that "if the Soviet Union continues to expand strategic forces, compensatory U.S. programs will be mandatory." [1] It is true that only some six or seven years ago Robert NcNamara was arguing that the Soviet Union did not aspire to strategic parity with the United States and was content with the smaller second-strike force as an effective deterrent to an American first strike. But, given the vast second-strike capability which the United States in fact maintains, I find it hard to see how any level of Soviet strategic power, except of a size that would bankrupt the country, can seriously threaten American security, and this view seems to have been ratified by the SALT treaty, signed by the President and Leonid Brezhnev in May 1972. It is possible that this change in the ratio of strategic power may be inducing a new sense of confidence in the Soviet elite and impressing other countries also with the dynamism of Soviet external policy, but there is no conclusive evidence of this so far.

Moreover, whatever the ratios between the two great strategic powers, this is still a level of power which is effectively bipolar, as the framework of the SALT negotiations has

[1] *Foreign Policy Report, 1972*, p. 179.

illustrated. China may be patiently and methodically developing a strategic force, at vast cost to her general advancement as a technological power; but thus far her record of progress has been slower than predicted by many Western and Soviet experts, and Chou En-lai has stated explicitly that "China will never be a superpower." France and Britain may have effective nuclear capabilities, though Paris and London are at this moment equally uncertain about their long-term future. Despite the existence of the Nonproliferation Treaty, quiet men in the back rooms of Japanese universities and research institutes may be doing sums about the technicalities and costs of a national nuclear force should the need arise, and they probably have their counterparts in Tel Aviv, Canberra, Cape Town, and New Delhi. But, if a crisis were to occur again at one or another junction of the two great alliance systems, which might conceivably imply recourse to nuclear weapons, the world, for the foreseeable future at any rate, would immediately re-polarize around Washington and Moscow, or stand mute in impotence until the crisis had been sweated out between them. I do not say that in a situation of parity the United States would necessarily be able to act nowadays with quite the same speed and decisiveness as Kennedy acted a decade ago over Cuba, especially if it were in an area close to the Soviet Union rather than, as in 1962, on the doorstep of the United States. What I am saying is that in a strategic nuclear crisis there would be no substitute for American decisions, no alternative Western actor. I am not sure that what remains of the Sino-Soviet alliance would stand up beneath the strain of such a crisis; but I think Peking's understanding of the risks of nuclear conflict has increased, and I doubt if it would now rain curses on Moscow's head as it did during and after the Cuban crisis.

I will come back to the question of strategic power, for it will affect some of our assumptions about the next twenty years. For the time being it is sufficient to note two points: First, that the development of an awareness of parallel Soviet-American interests during the ten years since the Cuban crisis, in the sense of both tacit and explicit understanding about the rules by which deterrence can be maintained while war may be avoided, has led neither to a superpower condominium, as the French and the Chinese feared throughout the 1960s, nor to a significant expansion of the area of political détente, even though the subjects on the agenda of East-West discussion, such as technology, health and trade, have widened. Second, the Non-proliferation Treaty, the only normative instrument successfully imposed by the superpowers, is still a fragile affair, many of whose complex technical provisions on inspection have yet to be negotiated. At the same time, the first stage of a SALT agreement has proved to be rather a modest affair. The communiqué after President Nixon's visit to Moscow has shown that it will have little linkage with such specific sources of superpower tension as the Middle East, or with rational arms control measures such as mutual force reduction in Central Europe, let alone a solution to the Indochina conflict. The existence of two superpowers, despite the greater facility of their communication, has not produced a new world order, as many Americans and some Europeans like John Strachey or Raymond Aron thought it might. The bipolar relationship remains primarily an adversary one.

At the second level of conventional, tactical, deployable, or usable military force, considerable changes are occurring —if measured purely in terms of capabilities. The United States is by intent reducing herself from the military status of a superpower to that of a large power. When she has moved over to a system of zero-draft or, as we call it, to regular forces—as indeed for social reasons she must—the capability of the United States to support all but her key alliances with deployed land and air forces must be questionable. It was, I think, a little unrealistic ever to talk of a capability to fight two and a half wars. Now what will be at issue will be the ability or the readiness of the United States to provide forces beyond her borders, high quality forces, on the terrain of certain key allies, in Germany, in the Mediterranean, in Korea, in Japan, in order to maintain confidence in the face of adversary pressure and to provide flexibility and restraint in a local crisis. It is a function that cannot be performed centrally, from Omaha or from Washington, if the United States is to remain the leader of a broad system of alliances and if the credibility of the American strategic guarantee to them is to be maintained; it may be a difficult function to sustain over the next decade and beyond. It is one thing for the Nixon Doctrine to state that henceforward allies must bear a greater share of the burden of local deterrence, a view with which few of the Pacific or European allies can quarrel. It is a rather different matter to translate this into terms of practical shifts of responsibility, especially in an era when manpower costs are soaring throughout the democratic industrial powers and public resources of all kinds are scarce among the less developed allies. In this forthcoming shift of emphasis we must expect that the political coherence of the Western alliance systems will suffer some, though not necessarily irreparable, damage and that the United States will not play so central a part as hitherto in determining their general policies.

But it is important not to make the opposite mistake of thinking that, because the United States must now define her security interests more rigorously, at a time when there appears to be no comparable process at work in China or the Soviet Union, the power balance—that mysterious entity which I wish to examine more closely later—is somehow shifting against the West. In military terms, China remains what she has been for a decade, a static power with little ability to intervene beyond her borders and an intense preoccupation with the defense of her western and northern frontiers. In another ten or fifteen years, she may have built an effective air force (she is today the largest producer of fighter aircraft) and a modern navy, though as with strategic weapons this will be a serious drain on other forms of modernization. She appears still, however, to envisage this form of power in terms of her own security, rather than as endowing her with an ability to intervene or project military influence at any distance from her borders.

The new military capabilities of the Soviet Union can also be overrated: true, she has somewhat larger ground and tactical air forces deployed in Central Europe than she had four years ago, but she now has 33 divisions on the Chinese border where four years ago she had 15, which means that she has to find some 20 more mobilized divisions out of roughly the same pool of manpower. True, she has for ten years been building a modern surface and underwater navy where the Western powers have been largely concerned in overhauling theirs; true, her captains are beginning to acquire greater experience in long-range navigation than historically any Russian navy has possessed. She apparently sees diplomatic purposes for this naval power in certain oceans and in certain countries. But to argue from this that she is about to exert a new form of challenge to the West is to overlook several points: first, that the Soviet Union is becoming a major maritime power in every sense with large mercantile, fishing, and oceanographic as well as naval interests; second, that the days when gunboat diplomacy could be exercised with political impunity by major powers has, with the increasing political consciousness of the world community, diminished and perhaps disappeared; third, that in the most improbable contingency one can envisage, namely, a purely naval conflict between the Soviet Union and the Western allies, the latter possess a much more diverse and formidable armory than the former; and finally, thanks to the lucky accident that the Europeans powers took to the ocean roughly at the same time as the early development of international law, the freedom of the seas and the conduct of the powers upon them are governed by a stronger framework of normative rules and customs than almost any other area of human activity. To take fright at the prospect of half a dozen Soviet ships in the Indian Ocean, of a squadron in the Eastern Mediterranean (smaller and less well equipped than the Italian navy), or the occasional cruiser off the coast of South America is, first, to be guilty of a form of *hubris* which will bedevil our thinking about the new pattern of international equilibrium, namely, that the high seas are an exclusive Western possession; second, to act as an unpaid public relations officer for Fleet Admiral Gorshkov.

* * *

It is at the third level of national power, that of political or psychological influence, that the world of the 1970s appears to differ most markedly from that of the 1960s. If I start with the decline in American influence, it is not from any wish to turn the knife in the wound but because I think it is one of the most important elements in the new situation. If one thinks back to the world of ten years ago, one can recall that the United States was a superpower in a much more profound sense than merely the possessor of the largest armory of strategic weapons; she was, as McGeorge Bundy is said to have described her, "the engine of mankind." [2] She was, as she still is, not only the center of a system of alliances that were central to the security of every democratic industrial state, including Switzerland, Austria, and Sweden, and of many developing countries as well. More than that, she was the principal source of overseas aid, the driving force in technological and scientific innovation, the sheet anchor of the United Nations, the main fount of ideas in fields as various as econometrics and arms control. She was the great, and the greatly successful, experimental society of the world, the center of a liberal pragmatism in governmental and in social relations which made her, and in particular the great universities which stoked the boilers of the engine, the intellectual as well as the political hub of an international system that embraced the aligned and nonaligned countries alike, or at any rate their intellectual and political leaders.

As Isaiah Berlin pointed out many years ago, it was the social dynamism and economic success of the New Deal

[2] Henry F. Graff, "How Johnson Makes Foreign Policy," *The New York Times Magazine,* July 4, 1965.

which weaned my generation of Europeans, the students and intelligentsia of the 1930s, away from Marxism. It is not surprising that, when to the appeal which the egalitarianism and mobility of American society made was added the ability to wield great strategic and economic power, and when it became clear—as Truman, Eisenhower, and Kennedy each in their different ways made clear—that such power could be used with both firmness and restraint, her influence extended far beyond her formal commitments or her military strength. Nor was this simply at the level of governments: a society that could simultaneously produce Dr. Spock, Hyman Rickover, Marilyn Monroe, and Martin Luther King had something for everyone, whether a Yorkshire housewife, a German scientist, a Japanese teenager, or a Nigerian politician. An American friend concerned with the Alliance for Progress recalls that ten years ago every Brazilian peasant had two pictures in his hut, one of the Virgin Mary and one of John F. Kennedy.

I will not at this point attempt to explore the reasons why the United States has come, for the time being, to be regarded, in Europe, in Pacific Asia, in the developing world, less as the mainspring of civilization and more as the generator of crude power, because I wish first to note other ways in which the world is changing at the beginning of the second quarter-century after Hiroshima. First and foremost, one cannot fail to observe the extension of Soviet political interests in countries and continents adjacent to her borders, and the confidence that accompanies this extension. Among the most important developments of 1971, a year that for many reasons marked the watershed between one structure of international power and another, was the conclusion of the Soviet-Egyptian and Soviet-Indian treaties in May and August, respectively. Though these do not automatically commit the larger power to come to the aid of the smaller in the event of war, as our own Atlantic treaty did, they are the first such treaties of alliance the Soviet Union has made with a non-Communist power since the war. Certainly the Indian treaty is in part a reaction to the thaw in Sino-American relations, and it had a great deal to do with the subsequent Indian action over Bangladesh. Together they represent, I suggest, a formal ratification of the fact that the Soviet Union, which fifteen years ago had no coherent Middle Eastern policy and ten years ago no consistent policy for the subcontinent, has now successfully unbuckled the girdle of containment with which Secretary of State John Foster Dulles attempted to encircle her in the mid-1950s. These new bases of power are an aspect of the Soviet Union's recognition of the growing multipolarity of world politics—not a situation, I think, that she has favored but one which she nevertheless accepts.

One of her prime concerns is to develop her own containment strategy vis-à-vis China, whose superior appeal to the developing world she rightly fears. A key element of this strategy has been the evolution of an entente with India. But Russian policy-makers know that, given the formidable barrier of the Himalayas, any European state that wishes to exert influence in India must have a strong, even a dominant, position astride the communications nexus of the Middle East, as Britain had for about seventy years after 1880. In fact, the Soviet Union is pursuing a dual-purpose policy of encircling China, even to the point of hinting at a collective security arrangement with South and Southeast Asian countries, which at the same time dislocates long-standing Western interests and affiliations in the area.

If the Soviet Union has lately been more reasonable in her attitude toward Western Europe—her initialing of both a new Berlin agreement and a treaty which accepts the Federal Republic as a responsible member of the international community—this is not necessarily, as some Europeans argue, because she is becoming obsessed with China. The reason may be that she has become very concerned recently, after the Czech crisis, the Polish uprisings, and the successful maintenance of a semi-autonomous policy on the part of Rumania, with re-establishing her predominance in Eastern Europe. If, through a European Security Conference, she can extract formal Western recognition that Eastern Europe is her special sphere of influence, this for the time being represents a more important objective than disrupting the EEC, which Brezhnev has said that he accepts, even though the domination of all Europe is an eventual objective she will not readily renounce.

Despite the vastness of her military establishment, despite her effort to achieve nuclear parity with the United States, despite her new naval and marine capabilities, and despite her new alliances, the Soviet Union remains, I think, as cautious as ever in her attitude to the actual use of her own force beyond the perimeter she has established. Her interest beyond the perimeter is in control, not ownership, whether it be Gulf oil, or Asian and eventually Western European capitals. If, for instance, she can keep Arab resolution to the sticking point long enough, she may emerge as the eventual arbiter of the Arab-Israel balance; if, by the same token, she comes to be accepted as the guardian of the new power balance in the subcontinent, the conciliator between President Bhutto and Sheikh Mujib as well as the ally of India, she will have achieved a striking extension of her political power. For, in a world of fast-moving events, when the earlier diplomatic successes of the United States, or genuine Chinese support for genuine liberation movements, may have been forgotten, she can reasonably hope to stand before the world, especially the Third World, both as the great peacemaker, even though she may also be one of its greatest suppliers of armaments, and as the most dynamic actor on the international stage. It is an imperial not an ideological conception of her national interest.

My knowledge of China is necessarily derivative, but I do not have the sense that she has as ambitious a concept of her national interest as the Soviet Union. She knows that she has not the capabilities of a superpower and will not have them for decades to come. Her long land border with Russia, her sense of ancient and modern wrongs to her territorial sovereignty, her knowledge of being sur-rounded by states more powerful than herself give her an obsession with territorial security which I think may be just beginning to disappear from the higher levels of Russian thought. Her leaders are aware of the failures of a more activist policy in the past—in Indonesia, for instance. Yet all that I have read of Chinese policy and Chinese state-ments makes me feel that, not only does she legitimately regard herself as a great power, relatively poor though she may be, but the demonstrable ability of her leaders to pull a shattered country up by its own bootstraps, the austerity and rigor of her domestic planning, the fact that she has been the poor relation of the modern great powers give her an opportunity for influence in the developing world, especially in far-away areas like East Africa or Latin America, which have no reason, as Asian states may have, to fear the pressure of her vast population. This may be a form of political influence which the industrial powers, including the Soviet Union, cannot match. The overwhelming support of the developing countries for China's admission to the General Assembly seems to provide some confirmation of this view.

But China remains a very difficult country for the outsider to interpret. Clearly President Nixon's visit has not been without influence on the thinking of her leaders. I have no doubt that Chou En-lai and his colleagues do not want a total American withdrawal from Asia even though they may have insisted upon it as far as Taiwan is concerned. Clearly the Soviet Union is what it has been for many years, the principal rival and adversary. What is obscure is whether China is determined to develop a second adversary relationship with Japan, or whether she can be brought to envisage Japan as a possible partner in the Asian power balance. China has had limited experience of participating in a multiple relationship with major powers—a brief and not very rewarding membership in the League of Nations, twenty-five years' exclusion from the United Nations, and only occasional contacts with the other major states in a multilateral setting, such as the Geneva Conference of 1954. However, like the other major powers, she seems to recognize the inevitability of such a multiple relationship in the future, whether it be trilateral, quadrilateral, or pentagonal in structure. But she stepped into a full role on the international scene in 1971, only a few years after one of the most curious internal upheavals in modern history, the Cultural Revolution, and only a few months after a conflict within the central leadership which led to the dismissal and subsequent death of Chairman Mao's specifically appointed successor. With a further change in the highest leadership inevitable before long, no one, I think, can assert with any confidence that he knows either who the new leaders will be or how they will interpret the Chinese interest in the new pattern of world politics which is emerging. It could be relatively limited and parochial; it could be more ambitious.

This brings me to the other uncertain political actors on the new world stage, Western Europe and Japan. It is not at all easy for Japan to assess her interests, because, for twenty years after the peace treaty that restored her sovereignty, she conceived them primarily in economic terms, though the demand for the return of Okinawa, national concern about the future of Taiwan and the Korean peninsula, and negotiations, so far abortive, about the recovery of Sakhalin and the Kuriles are political, not economic, issues. We are aware that there is an accelerating tempo of debate in Japan, sharpened by the developments of 1971, on her future role in the world: whether she is the Eastern bastion of a multilateral Western system of security, economics, finance, government, and values; whether she must become a global power in political and military terms as she has become global in her economic interests; or whether she is primarily a Pacific and Oriental power which happens to possess a capitalist economic base but can play a mediatory and balancing role in the politics of Asia. I agree with Professor Brzezinski, who wrote recently that "the American side has not been fully responsive to the Japanese quest for higher status, and to the need to appeal to the more honorable and magnanimous side of the Japanese character."[3] And what is true of Americans is true of Europeans also.

Though there has been a mercurial quality in Japanese decision-making if looked at over the last century or so, there are certain fixed points discernible at present: a greater sense of cultural affinity with China than with the Soviet Union if a choice between them should become inevitable; a reluctance to face both the political risks and economic costs of the kind of rearmament which would give Japan a free hand in world politics, but an earnest desire to be accepted as a serious and senior member of the international community; a new sense of alarm at the autonomy which American policy now displays, coupled with an acknowledgment that she still has common interests with the United States on such questions as the future of Taiwan and South Korea; a growing involvement *malgré lui* in the political future and stability of such Southeast Asian countries as Indonesia, Malaysia, and Australia, where her economic involvement is now considerable; a new preoccupation with the social consequences of her rapid economic growth. I think the Japanese predicament can be summed up as one between growing national power and self-confidence parallel with a continuing sense of her economic and strategic vulnerability—as an economic superpower, for instance, which has few indigenous resources or raw materials.

The case of Western Europe is quite different. Here is a

[3] "Japan's Global Engagement," *Foreign Affairs*, January 1972.

group of countries which together have a very wide variety of political interests in the world at large but which have not yet tackled the problem of reconciling them where they may conflict. They have not yet created the machinery for such coordination; and their power to protect even those interests which are eventually identified as central is likely to remain limited. One can now be sure that the members of the European Community, which will include Britain and possibly Denmark and Norway as well, will set about in earnest trying to identify a priority of common interests. The Gaullist "ice age," the attempt to identify a mysterious European *persona* with France, or ideas about a purely indigenous Soviet-European balance are things of the past.

But a number of factors, only partly within the control of the Western European governments themselves, will decide the pace of this process, and the conclusions that will eventually emerge. One will be an answer to the question of whether the development of a European consensus at the fourth level of power, the monetary and economic, will have to be given priority over the coordination of other political interests—for there may not be enough leadership and common purpose in the next few years to tackle both problems simultaneously. Another will be the extent to which the countries of the Community as a whole discern an indefinite continuation of the American interest in the security of Western Europe that has been a feature of the past twenty-five years. If a serious doubt about this should arise or persist, it will profoundly affect both the structure of the new Europe and the definition of its interests. Yet another factor will be the extent to which special European interests—maintaining the substance of the *Ostpolitik,* for instance, or preventing conflict and political decadence in the Mediterranean—may have to be given priority over broader concerns. Finally there is the question of how the new institutions and mechanisms which can effectively co-ordinate, let alone control, the exercise of Western European influence in the world are to be created, accepted, and made to work.

If Japan is a tentative newcomer to a modern multiple balance of power in the world, Europe is still a diffuse one. Discussions on the next step forward have thus far gone no further than modest suggestions for providing the Council of Ministers with a permanent secretariat and expanding the influence of the European Parliament. True, the informal Eurogroup of NATO Defense Ministers has been able to make certain modest proposals to the United States in the field of burden-sharing; but the question of whether a European identity that will include France can be established in the defense field is quite unsolved. True, there is considerable confidence that the European Community will gradually identify a series of external political interests, most though not all of which should be complementary to American interests. But Europe's interests may by no means be universal, even if those of Britain and France have been global in the past; and the process of evolving consensus even on more limited ones cannot take place overnight, whether despite American policy or because of it. Western Europe is not going to acquire the attributes of a super-power in the near future, despite the fact that it includes two nuclear powers; perhaps it never will. Like Japan, the countries of which the Community is composed are strategically vulnerable; like Japan, they are dependent on far-off sources of power and raw materials; and, though they have now a generation's experience of various forms of co-operation, this does not endow them—unlike Japan—with the characteristics of a unitary state. I am certain that they will act henceforth with increasing community of purpose on the international scene, but the problems of coexistence with an adversary coalition on their own continent are get-ting no easier to solve and may be their central preoccupa-tion. Yet, though they remain her military allies and her economic partners, it is no longer possible to regard the countries of the Community simply as an extension of the United States—and in this generalization I include Great Britain.

*   *   *

The changes that have occurred in the distribution of political influence are in part related to changes in the relative economic power of the major capitals. The postwar monetary and trade system, the International Monetary Fund (IMF), and the General Agreement on Tariffs and Trade (GATT) were founded on the assumption of an American economic dominance which would make the U.S. dollar the world's basic currency and would enable the United States to accept low tariff barriers in return for reciprocal action on the part of her industrial allies. Twenty years ago the United States produced half the world's wealth; but now she produces less than a third despite the fact that she still is by far the largest, and in many ways the most dynamic, economic power in the world. The growth of Soviet economic power, though striking, has done no more than keep pace with that of America (Russia's GNP is about half that of her fellow superpower), while China exerts only limited economic influence in the world. The most striking change of the past decade has been the growth in the economy and the economic influence of Japan plus that of certain European countries, notably Germany.

These changes have not occurred overnight. Indeed, the whole of the past decade has been fraught with monetary crises among the non-Communist powers as the second international currency, sterling, got into increasing difficulties and an over-all deficit in the American balance of payments, which had started in the late 1950s, turned out to be not temporary but endemic. Various expedients initiated by either the United States or the Group of Ten (Belgium, Britain, Canada, France, Germany, Italy, Japan, Netherlands, Sweden, United States) have had only short-lived success. The increasing fluctuations in the gold market were temporarily subdued by the organization of a Gold Pool, but that fell apart in 1968 when the market price of gold was separated from the official price at which the United States would sell gold. In 1967 the growing weakness of sterling was remedied by the devaluation of the pound. In 1969 the uneasiness of the world's foreign exchange markets was temporarily allayed by the devaluation of the franc and the revaluation of the Deutsche mark.

But these expedients did not solve the fundamental problems which have come to confront the United States: a very high level of external investment on the part of American companies and banks; a continuing debit in the country's official accounts as a consequence of overseas aid and the stationing of troops abroad (despite force reductions in Vietnam); and a steady expansion in the rest of the world's short-term credit assets denominated in dollars. Together these three factors have combined to make the American position different from that of any other powerful industrial nation.

What differentiates the exercise of power and its interaction among powerful states on the economic, as contrasted with the political or strategic, plane is its relationship to domestic considerations such as inflation and unemployment, and thus to domestic politics. Policy on the other planes may become a burning domestic issue, as the Suez adventure became in Britain for a short while in 1956 or the Vietnam war in the United States for longer. But, for the most part, strategic and foreign policy in general is not the day-to-day stuff of electoral politics to the extent that questions such as unemployment, prosperity, and the cost of living are. It is not surprising, therefore, that democratic governments feel tempted to put their countries' own economic interests ahead of wider considerations of the general well-being or of the solidarity of alliances if the agreed rules of international trade and finance become maladjusted to the realities of the situation. It happened in the periods of economic depression in the nineteenth century; it happened in the 1930s. Thus it is difficult to blame President Nixon for feeling that the United States was in a serious crisis when it became clear by the spring of 1971 that administrative efforts to control the outflow of American investment had had only a marginal effect and that the American balance-of-payments deficit was running at twice the record $10.7 billion deficit of the previous year. Whether shock tactics, the imposition on August 15, 1971, of a heavy surcharge on industrial imports and the divorce of the dollar from its gold standard, without consultation with the industrial trading partners of the United States and with her co-adjutors in maintaining of the international monetary system, were the right way to make the necessary adjustment is, however, very much open to question by reason of the interaction—which is constant—between the economic and the political planes of power, influence, and confidence.

It is true that, by the end of 1971, the objective of these shock tactics—a significant revaluation of the other major currencies in relation to the dollar, thus making American domestic products more competitive with foreign imports and discouraging the outflow of American investment dollars—had been substantially achieved. But at a considerable price. First, it has shaken Japanese confidence in the durability of a close economic relationship with the United States, though Japan, whose penetration of the American consumer market was responsible for about 40 per cent of the over-all deficit of the United States and 70 per cent of its trade deficit in the first half of 1971, might well have been more alert to the political complications this was creating for the President. Second, although there was little unity of policy or action in Europe in the monetary field during the crises before 1971, particularly between France and Germany, the effect of the President's shock tactics has been to hasten a European consensus that the development of a unified or closely coordinated European monetary system may have to be given priority over the renovation of wider multilateral institutions like the IMF. This is a view now shared as much by the British as by the governments of the Six, and it is significant that President Pompidou, meeting with President Nixon at the end of 1971, felt (after prior consultation with Chancellor Brandt) in a position to speak for Europe as a whole, even though the European governments had not reacted identically to the American challenge in August.

Nevertheless, those who direct the governments of the industrial powers have memories of the 1930s, when inflation and unemployment, today's symptoms in most industrial democracies, led to competitive devaluations and rising tariff barriers. Today, governments in Europe and in the Pacific have greater reason to fear a new era of American isolationism than in the interwar years, so there is a readiness to make adjustments in both trade and monetary questions which was lacking then; the Smithsonian agreement of December 1971 was the first effort to put Humpty Dumpty together again. There is also a much clearer recognition of the relationship between international politics and economics—that "political economy" is not an archaic term —than there was a generation ago. But, at a time when the flow of dollars back and forth across the oceans is seen to be much more the product of market forces or the individual decisions of private banks or multinational corporations than of official policy, when the general phenomena of inflation plus unemployment create a continuous temptation to put domestic interests first, when it has become clear that the EEC and Japan have proportionately much larger reserves than the United States and that her freedom of action is thus relatively limited, the problems of reconciling domestic and international priorities could, unless we can count on a high order of statesmanship in most of the industrial powers, lead to continuous frictions of not only economic but political significance. Just as the end of the cold war has led to an end of the simple values of right and wrong, them versus us, in international politics, so the relatively simple era of American dominance at all levels of power is disappearing also. One obvious danger is that this sense of malaise about the future of the international monetary and trade systems, put together with difficulty in the postwar years and maintained with ever greater difficulty into the 1960s, may lead to false political judgments or attempted short cuts, such as the withdrawal of all American forces not only from the Pacific but from Europe, even though this is only a minor factor in the adverse balance of American payments.

It would be foolish for a non-economist to propound solutions to this malaise.[4] But someone who is concerned to look at the changing distribution of power may legitimately ask whether the other two major political actors, the Soviet Union and China, are likely to become involved in this differentiation of interests among the major Western power centers. On a minor key, of course, they already are. Trade between Western Europe and Eastern Europe and the Soviet Union increases steadily though not dramatically; the West European powers and, even more, Japan have a useful level of trade with China. The significant consideration is, I think, that both the Soviet Union and, at a lower level, China have a thirst for the products and patents that are an outcome of American, European, and Japanese research and technological processes. All the Western actors are bound, therefore, to ask themselves whether they cannot to some

[4] For two excellent analyses of the implications of the dollar crisis of 1971, see "The New Economics and U.S. Foreign Policy," by C. Fred Bergsten, *Foreign Affairs,* January 1972, and "The Dollar Crisis 1971," by Susan Strange, *International Affairs,* April 1972.

extent redress the problems they have encountered in their relations with each other by new trade and technological relationships with Moscow or Peking. The return they receive might, so they may calculate, as usefully take the form of political adjustments (concessions on transnational movements, for instance, or, in the case of Japan, on the future ownership of territory left undecided by the postwar era of confrontation) as new markets or sources of raw materials. If the purchasing power of the developing world is likely to remain quite limited, if the growth of trade within the Western industrial world is going to encounter serious and permanent national obstacles by reason of the need to protect and stimulate domestic employment, if overseas markets are going to be an endemic problem in the final quarter of this century as they were not in its third quarter, then there is likely to be a hankering for new arrangements across the Elbe or the China Sea.

* * *

Before turning to ask what the forces are that are making our contemporary world so different from that to which we became accustomed in the postwar years, I would like to touch briefly on three other aspects of a changing scene. In the years of the cold war when the structure of physical and economic power was effectively bipolar, many people argued that there was in reality a third factor to the balance, namely, the nonaligned powers, the Third World, the Afro-Asian Bloc—the name varied according to who was attempting to define it. As British, French, Dutch, and Belgian decolonization continued, a group of new states emerged, led for the most part by men who declared high principles, who expressed a determination to stand aloof from the "power politics" of the Western and Eastern camps. If they were not the balancing element of world politics in any physical sense, they felt that they represented a new "conscience of mankind" and could exert a moral influence both by their unity and by their noninvolvement in the power struggles of the northern hemisphere. And this was not wholly an illusion. The industrial powers took account of the Bandung spirit; the role played by India in the negotiations for the end of the Korean war, in the Indochina crisis of 1954, in the Suez crisis (where, it is true, the Western camp itself was divided) was far from negligible.

But this unity and this influence no longer exist. The successors to two of the great apostles of nonalignment, Jawaharlal Nehru and Gamal Abdel Nasser, have led their countries into alliances with the Soviet Union, leaving only Marshal Tito, obsessed with the internal problems of Yugoslavia and fearful of Soviet intervention in them when he goes, as the survivor of a once powerful trinity. Sukarno is dead, and Nkrumah died in exile, leaving their successors to cope with mountainous debts and problems. India is deeply involved in the power politics of the subcontinent; Egypt, in those of the Middle East; and the ramifications of the Arab-Israel hostilities penetrate deep into Africa. The hope of many Asians and Africans and some Westerners like Malcolm Macdonald and Chester Bowles that the developing world would acquire the unity to act as a subject rather than an object of world politics has been belied.

The rise of military regimes, often through violent *coups d'état*, throughout Asia and Africa as well as Latin America has weakened the moral position of the Third World. Latin

America itself can no longer be considered a political unit, whether anti- or pro-American. While the grinding poverty of most developing countries is, as Lester Pearson stressed in the previous Leffingwell Lectures, a problem that touches the consciences of us all, they can no longer be lumped together even in economic terms. Taiwan and South Korea, Iran and Kuwait, Nigeria, Malaysia, Libya, and Singapore have a different magnitude of resources at their command than, say, Chad and Dahomey, Burma or Ethiopia.

Second, if the nonaligned world has ceased to be the conscience of the aligned, by the same token the United Nations has ceased, for the time being, to be the instrument for moderating conflicts among either the great powers or the lesser. As McGeorge Bundy put it in a recent speech in London:

> The limited influence of distant power is reflected not only in the actual behavior of the great states, but also in the steadily declining role of the United Nations as the arbiter of conflict. The U.N. may have been right or wrong to have engaged itself so heavily in the Congo in the early 1960's—but by the end of the decade no one any longer expected that it would be the centre of action in such a case again. Even in the Middle East, where perhaps it had had its largest single historic role, the U.N. by the end of the decade was reduced to the honourable but marginal role of providing a skilled and silent diplomatic messenger.[5]

How much of this decline in the political influence of the United Nations is a consequence of the refusal of the United States to associate it in any way with the conflict

[5] Stevenson Memorial Lecture, Chatham House, November 30, 1971.

in Vietnam, I am not prepared to speculate, having been only a distant observer during the crucial years. I intend to discuss later the centrality of the United Nations—of which China is now a member and to which I hope the two Germanys will shortly be admitted—to the operation of a modern multiple balance-of-power system. For the time being, however, one can only note that the United Nations as a means of institutionalizing the use of power is at the nadir of success.

The third way in which the relations of the major states have come to differ in the past five years from those of the previous twenty concerns, on the one hand, the internal coherence of their own societies and, on the other, their readiness to promote incoherence in the societies of smaller states, allies of their adversaries, or to restrain it in those of their own allies.

The political and social unity which great states have been able to maintain and demonstrate has been a traditional factor in any calculus of the balance of power. It was the uncertainty about the loyalty which Vienna could command among her heterogeneous subject peoples which weakened the diplomatic hand of Austria-Hungary after the middle of the nineteenth century and diminished the autonomy and respect to which the human and physical resources within her borders would have otherwise entitled her. Much the same could be said of Imperial Russia between 1880 and 1917. In the first twenty years or so after 1945, civil violence between governments and dissident ethnic or social groups, or between different tribes or interests, was primarily a characteristic of the developing world, first in conflict with colonial powers, then domestically. But, with the rise of a new generation to articulate political influence, it has become, though in a more muted and controlled fashion, a feature of the developed world. This has been most marked in the United States, where the change coincided with an unsuccessful overseas expedition whose burden was born most directly by the rising generation. But the conflict, inherent in generation change in an era of mass education and mass communications, has been evident in Japan and the continental countries of Western Europe as well. At the same time, the fashion for civil violence, which though it originated in Europe has not been manifest there for some time, has given a new and keen edge of bitterness to the communal problems of Great Britain's Irish province, just as to Quebec's search for cultural and political autonomy within the Canadian federal system. In China the causes and consequences of the Cultural Revolution are so difficult to discern that it is hard to assess with any confidence whether Peking feels it can now count on the unquestioned loyalty of its hundreds of millions of young and adult subjects. Of the major actors, only the Soviet Union presents (despite the opposition of a small band of brave and devoted intellectuals) a façade of unbroken national unity to the world.

Does this mean that there is a fifth plane, of relative national unity and of the authority of government within its own society, on which relative power and autonomy must be examined and measured? Very possibly, though the technique of measurement might daunt even the most quantitatively minded sociologist, given the incalculable factors of circumstance, personality, and leadership. Moreover, it might be a task of diminishing relevance to international politics. The rise of social violence in the developed world has coincided with a diminishing interest on the part of both the Communist and the Western powers in intervening in the social and political conflicts of the Third World except where their own primary interests might be directly affected: the Caribbean as concerns the United States, Eastern Europe as concerns the Soviet Union, her whole long border as concerns China, conceivably Korea as concerns Japan. The quiet American acceptance of the Allende regime in Chile, the refusal of the Soviet Union to become involved in the civil conflict in the Sudan despite Egypt's entreaties, the abstention of China from attempting to repeat its involvement in the politics of Indonesia are cases in point. In 1971 every interested foreign power, including Britain, the United States, the Soviet Union, and eventually China, came to the aid of Mrs. Sirimavo Bandaranaike in defeating a Trotskyite rebellion in Ceylon. As Pierre Hassner has expressed it:

> One is then tempted to see a succession of three patterns since the war. First there was the bipolar international civil war, where every civil conflict seemed part of the Soviet-American war. Second, Soviet Russia progressively shifted to an interstate approach and to a preference for stability, with China taking over the flag of revolution. Third, China too, emerging as a 'mature power,' is now playing predominantly a balance-of-power game, mixing competition with 'Holy Alliance' and 'concert-of-powers' aspects when it happens to share an interest in stability with its rivals.[6]

[6] "Civil Violence and the Pattern of International Peace," in *Civil Violence and the International System*, Adelphi Paper No. 83, ISS, London, 1971.

This may be too broad or too early a generalization, but I think it is fair to say that a multiple power balance is re-emerging at a time when all the major participants in it are more politically introverted, more concerned with the organization, order, and prosperity of their own large societies and social systems, less disposed to impose their standards on others, with less energy available for scoring a point off their adversaries, than was the case in the 1950s and 1960s.

Why is it that our assumptions about the new structure of the international system are now so different from those of a few years ago—or, to be more precise, why do I find my own assumptions so different? I think there are many causes; and it is not, as some Americans believe, merely a consequence of one socially disastrous war, nor even of the decline of the external luster of American society—of a change, as Archibald MacLeish once described it, in "the feel of America in the world's mind"; of a recognition that engines can go into neutral or reverse as well as forward. If one thinks back to the world of the early 1960s—to President Kennedy's conception in 1962 of the Atlantic Alliance as one of "twin pillars," one American, one European; to the final Sino-Soviet rift of a year later; to the accumulating evidence even then of Japanese economic strength— one can detect the emergence of a plural world with several major power centers. Its evolution was delayed, as Richard Lowenthal has put it, "by an odd detour of history." [7] A decade ushered in by "the spirit of Camp David," with its emphasis on peaceful coexistence, which was expected to witness a decline in ideological and military rivalry, became

[7] "A World Adrift," *Encounter*, February 1972.

dominated in fact by military considerations and by ideological quarrels within both the Western and Eastern camps.

First the United States became more and more deeply engrossed in an overseas expedition which, since it seemed impossible to win, was increasingly credited to the intervention of external powers—notably in the Johnson era to the People's Republic of China. Because of some rather spurious comparisons with a similar British problem in Malaysia in the early postwar years, the U.S. Government began to credit China with a range of Machiavellian skills in intervention through subversion, as well as with limitless ambition, at the very moment when China herself was entering a period of internal trauma and preoccupation which made her for several years a nonmember of the international dialogue. Yet, though China may have been unable or unwilling to seek a more candid conversation with the United States, her challenge to the Soviet Union made Khrushchev's successors increasingly determined to consolidate their control over what they had, namely, over Eastern Europe, and to exert increasing influence in the Middle East and Southern Asia.

At roughly the same time (that is, in the first half of the 1960s), a chain of circumstances more related to the personality of Khrushchev than to the necessary interaction of the great powers (I mean the Cuban and Berlin crises) led to increasing preoccupation with the problems of security and crisis management, and so to a quite genuine dubiety in the United States as to the extent to which she could share decisions about the first level of power—strategic power—with her allies. This in turn led to the increased influence of President de Gaulle. But, as Lowenthal has written, de Gaulle "was fatally hampered in his drive for the realistic objective of a more independent role for Western Europe by his commitment to an irrelevant national ideology, which caused him to isolate his country and foil the progress of European unification by sterile attacks on the United States and by his veto of British entry into the Community." [8]

I hope I have said enough to impart my personal conviction that a plural world of five, possibly more, centers of major international power and influence is re-emerging. I could offer a string of American quotations from Thomas Jefferson to William James to Henry Kissinger to illustrate that this is not an alien concept to the American view of the world.[9] Why did the United States intervene in the two world wars if not to prevent the domination of Europe by a hegemonial power? What was American pressure for universal decolonization instead of confronting the Soviet Union by means of an American-British-French entente in 1947–48 other than a consequence of a conviction of the validity of pluralism? If the original impetus behind the American drive for European unity was a utilitarian one, to make her containment of the Soviet Union in Central Europe less onerous and more effective, it developed in the ensuing two decades into a very positive desire for a partner with whom to share America's concerns and burdens—a general attitude that has later been extended to Japan. The position of the Soviet Union, with her earlier nervousness

[8] *Ibid.*
[9] E.g., William James: "The world is in so far forth a pluralism of which the unity is not fully experienced as yet." *Essays in Radical Empiricism* (Longman's, 1912), p. 89.

about an intimate relationship with any other country, even her fellow superpower, her continuing preoccupation with control in Central Europe, and her obsession with the ideological and national conflict with China, makes a striking contrast.

The long-term objective of American postwar policy, a plural world of many states with more than two great ones, has to a large extent been realized, although no one, even after the beginning of the nuclear age, had foreseen the exponential growth in the development of power itself—strategic and military power, economic power, the power to influence and repel. We have lived before, and lived fruitfully, in a multipolar political and economic system, in "a balance of power." It is, therefore, worthwhile attempting to contrast the classic conceptions and requirements of such a system with the new restraints which the world of the later twentieth century imposes on its operation.

II

The Relevance of the Past

So far we have not progressed far beyond a glimpse of the obvious, namely, that the bipolar structure of the international system is dissolving before our eyes, but in different ways at different levels of power. The ownership of effective strategic nuclear power and therefore the control of events in the kind of crisis which might conceivably imply its use are still bipolar; this is a more important fact than the relative size of the Soviet-American strategic forces. Although there is an apparent shift in the ratio of conventional military power between the United States and the Soviet

Union, this is less significant than a gradual shift in the balance of political influence as the former appears likely to be able to contribute less to the collective forces of her key military alliances, while the latter has recently shown herself ready to take on new alliance commitments. While the United States must expect her major allies to pursue more autonomous policies than in the past, especially as her civilization ceases to command the excitement and moral allegiance of the younger half of their electorates, the Soviet Union seems anxious to remain predominant within her alliances, using her new ones to pursue a policy that both contains Chinese influence and disorients established Western interests, especially in Asia. Finally, I noted that at the level of economic power and influence the Western system is at present in disarray. Whether the interdependence of the Bretton Woods system, based on the centrality of the U.S. dollar and the dominance of the American economy, can be restored, at a time when Japan has larger reserves than the United States and the EEC countries have reserves three times as large as those of the United States, is a question not yet answered.

In other words there are now five major centers of military, political, or economic influence in the industrial world, each of which has different kinds of opportunities and restraints at different levels of power, both in relation to the others and in relation to the Third World, whose own moral and political unity has been eroded by time and circumstance. This was a situation which many people in government, the academic world, and journalism assumed was approaching in the early 1960s, only to see the pattern of significant power and interaction become largely frozen for eight years or so by a series of partly fortuitous circumstances.

World politics has only for short periods been governed by a simple bipolar balance of power, and these have mostly been times of active or impending war. We are, therefore, in a normal historical situation in which—insofar as physical analogies are illuminating rather than misleading—the balance of power resembles not a pair of scales but a mobile, which at different horizontal levels has a varying number of vertical components of different weights, the whole system being in a constant state of gentle movement and vibration. In consequence, it is useful to consider how statesmen and thinkers have operated and analyzed multiple systems of this kind in the past, what rules and assumptions have made the system work, and what causes have led to its downfall, so that—aware as we are of the titanic changes that have occurred in weapons and communications, in economic and political systems, over the past two generations—we can make some assessment of the areas where historical experience is relevant and those in which we must be prepared to improvise.

I should like to leave for the moment the direct application of these conceptions to the world of the 1970s and 1980s and to concentrate here on a somewhat more abstract and academic aspect of my theme. First of all, what did men perceive as the assumptions, the objectives, and the modalities of the classic European balance-of-power system, particularly in the nineteenth century, when the international system was, like our own, no longer homogeneous (to use Raymond Aron's phrase) since two of the five major actors, Britain and France, were liberal democracies and three, Russia, Austria, and Prussia, were autocracies? Then I think it useful to discuss the many meanings that this equivocal metaphor "the balance of power" has acquired and those that are relevant to our own day; closing, as becomes a visitor from a country that has been proud of its role in the maintenance of international equilibrium to a country that has been more skeptical than enthusiastic about the concept of a multiple balance, with some suggestions about the way in which Americans have looked and are looking at it.

The balance of power is a relatively modern conception. Of course, it is fun to read Thucydides and to find echoes of our own anxieties in the maneuvering of the Greek cities. In the same way, the relationships of Florence, Milan, and Venice, each with its various allies, present an interesting example of a tripolar relationship whose units neither trusted nor wished to destroy each other. But the level of power was so modest as to have little contemporary relevance, and in every case the three were part of a larger structure of states to which their rivalry eventually made them subordinate. The seventeenth century ought to have useful lessons to teach us—dominated like our own age by a bitter ideological conflict in the first half of the century and then by the necessary containment of an expansionist France toward the end. But, though our modern notion of the secular sovereign state emerged from its conflicts, power was so out of joint that for the most part men hoped to regain equilibrium by refederating Christendom—as, on a secular basis, we hoped to do the same in 1919 and in 1945 —rather than by balancing its components.

The eighteenth century, after the Treaty of Utrecht of

1713, which stated the restoration and maintenance of the balance of power as one of its objectives, is the classic era of European equilibrium, the period when it was clear beyond doubt that the modern secular state had come to stay, when power was fairly evenly distributed, and when the European state system had no real political perimeter. Once the Turkish Empire had been contained, there was no outside power that could overwhelm Europe; the only other major power system, China, was a moon's journey away. It was a complex international system, for, counting all the little bishoprics and dukedoms, there were probably some 300 more or less sovereign entities, double the number of sovereign states in the world today. It was a Europe dominated by fear of return to the chaos and barbarism of the previous century, as our world is today dominated by a fear of return to general war; and if thinkers and statesmen had not considered the requirements of order, there would have been no intellectual foundations on which to build a new international system after Napoleon had completely disrupted the old one.

One can, if one chooses, paint the eighteenth and nineteenth centuries' balance-of-power systems as a kind of cynical chess game between dynastically linked princes, using territory as pawns, occasionally moving off the European chess board altogether to maintain the balance of conflict or adjustment in North America or India. But, if one looks at the underlying assumptions, I think one can discern more relevance to our current concerns than might appear at first glance. For one thing, the system assumed the existence of a number of sovereign states of unequal power and interests; that too is our world, though the parameters of sovereignty have been narrowed by the existence of many functional international organizations. For another, it assumed that the system operated throughout Europe and not merely in part of it, just as we now live in a global but finite international system—the shrinking globe so graphically portrayed by the moon shots, a conception that made Wendell Willkie and Henry Wallace seem ridiculous when they talked about "one world" even a generation ago. True, there was for a while confusion and dissension as to whether Turkey was part of the European system, just as there was about China and the international system in the 1950s and early 1960s. But in the 1970s there is no argument about the universality of the international system. China is now part of it and so is Chad. Even such self-willed hermits of international society as South Africa cannot escape its influence. There is no conceivable outside threat to it, unless the *Pioneer* rocket should find and arouse some hostile civilization in the cosmos, to rally us into a terrestrial unity —Gabon and Colombia, Belgium and the Maldive Islands, North Korea and the Irish Free State—as first the Persians and then the Macedonians created a temporary unity of action among the rival Greek city-states. Some people clearly hope that the ecological threat and the exponential growth of our demands on finite natural resources will unify mankind in this way. Thus far, the evidence is lacking.

But several assumptions of the classical system seem less relevant nowadays: first of all, the homogeneity of the European states system or, as Burke put it, the fact that "no citizen of Europe could be altogether an exile in any part of it." And he became even more emphatic on this point the more he thought about it.

In the intercourse between nations we are apt to rely too much on the instrumental part . . . men are not tied to one another by paper and seals. They are led to associate by resemblances, by conformities, by sympathies. It is with nations as with individuals. Nothing is so strong a tie of amity between nation and nation as correspondence in laws, customs, manners, and habits of life. . . . The secret unseen but irrefragable bond of habitual intercourse holds them together, even when their perverse and litigious nature sets them to equivocate, scuffle, and fight about the terms of their written obligations.[1]

It is a difficult conception to accept today, when yellow men, black men, and white men seem to glare at each other across state frontiers, when not just states but civilizations confront each other, when governments have powers to create barriers to transnational movements which even the most vicious tyrannies then lacked. Yet what was the eighteenth century's concentration on the art of diplomacy directed at if not at overcoming similar obstacles, for we are apt to forget the enormous popular suspicion in those days of treating alien civilizations like Russia and Turkey as ordinary European states. Are not modern developments like mass communications, erratically and unevenly, creating these "irrefragable bonds"? There *is* an international social consciousness, whether it works at any given moment to our benefit or detriment, and whether it overrides the interests of the powerful states or not. I think some of the documents in the Pentagon Papers show this clearly: the troubled men beside the Potomac were concerned at the United States's being revealed not just as weak in the eyes of the Soviet Union but as wrong in the eyes of the world.

[1] *Letters on a Regicide Peace.*

True, the notion of state power is much more difficult to grasp than at any time in the past, when it could be comprehended in terms of size of population, square miles of territory, or control of narrow waters. The computerized calculations of the outcome of a nuclear war between x number of missiles on one side and y on the other are, fortunately, only an analogue of reality itself. In terms of military power, we have passed through so many technological changes since 1945 that no one can say with confidence what the outcome of a military crisis—even at the non-nuclear level—would be even though we know the exact relative sizes of, say, our own and the Warsaw Pact tank and air forces in Europe. When undue confidence is placed in a new instrument of military power, it often proves misplaced—for instance, the relative failure of the helicopter in Vietnam as an instrument for the control of territory. Moreover, we can only guess at the balance of political power in the world until some initiative or crisis shows up its reality. Fortunately, however, we no longer live in a penumbra of suspicion about changes in relative economic power, as in the generation before 1914 and to a certain extent in the interwar years, for this is now better documented and more calculable.

In addition, there appears to have been one crucial difference between the old multiple system and any counterpart that could develop in the next decade or so: then, territory was regarded as transferable, at least among the major continental powers. This readiness or ability to engage in trade-offs of territory, which continued to be applicable in the Balkans until late in the nineteenth century (*vide* the Congress of Berlin in 1878), was continued until the First World War and beyond in Africa and the Arab world. Because government was a primitive art, it could be argued that to the governed it did not make a great deal of difference under whose flag they lived. In a world of intense nationalism, nowhere is this true today. Yet the difference may be more apparent than real if one thinks in terms of influence rather than ownership. If one considers the fluctuations of aid policies and objectives, there have been adjustments, not only explicitly between the Western powers but also implicitly between the Western and the Communist powers. The major powers today are more concerned, as Arnold Wolfers once put it, with milieu, not possession, goals—to create a climate that is favorable to extension of their influence rather than to annex territory.

A more significant, and indeed more hopeful, difference between the old and the new is that the major states now generate power within their own borders by planning, by saving, by brain power and innovation, by hard work, without the need to acquire more territory or a larger labor force. Every major state (with the possible exception of the Soviet Union, which is still rather preoccupied with numbers) is now concerned with controlling its population growth rather than expanding it as a form of power, which was the case even in our grandfathers' day. It is only in conflicts between some small, new states that the relationship of territory to population still has its classic significance; for instance, on the Horn of Africa.

If we turn from the assumptions of those who operated the system to their objectives, we find much similarity between then and now. The central object of the balance of power was to preserve the system itself. It was designed to ensure the survival of the significant units and, in the process of ensuring autonomy, to provide a reasonable guarantee of peace. Above all, no one power must ever become preponderant. That was the cardinal aim on which everyone—be he an idealist like Kant, who thought the balance of power could be gradually institutionalized, or a diplomat like Gentz, who saw it as a mobile and fluid system—wholeheartedly agreed. In a broadsheet published in London in 1741, about the year "balance of power" became a cant phrase in politics, the infant Europa is catechised:

Catechist: Tell me wherein consists the Safety of Europe?
  Europa: In this same Ballance of Power.
Catechist: What is it that generally causes War in her Bowels?
  Europa: It is occasion'd by the Ballance of Power being destroy'd.
Catechist: And how may that Ballance be destroy'd?
  Europa: That Ballance may be destroyed by Force or Fraud; by the Pusillanimity of some, and the Corruption of all.
Catechist: When any Potentate hath arriv'd to an exorbitant Share of Power, ought not the Rest to league together in order to reduce him to his due Proportion of it?
  Europa: Yes, certainly.—Otherwise there is but one Potentate, and the others are only a kind of Vassals to him.[2]

We know that there were great abuses of the system, the chief being the partition of Poland in the 1790s, which was designed to preserve the balance among Russia, Prussia, and

[2] Quoted in Edward Gulick, *Europe's Classic Balance of Power* (Cornell University Press, 1955).

Austria, three mutually hostile states in a triangular relationship—a situation which could possibly have a contemporary application in South or East Asia today. We
know that, as far as the purely West European powers were
concerned, the system developed a perennial tendency to
turn from the politics of compromise to those of compensation, to shift conflicts and adjustment away from the continent of Europe toward what Toynbee called "the open
spaces"—North America and South Asia in the eighteenth
century, East Asia and Africa later. We know that there
was an unresolved argument among its proponents, which
nearly brought Europe into conflict again a generation after
the Congress of Vienna, as to whether or not the balance-of-
power system was an instrument for the preservation of the
social and territorial status quo.

But, given the position in which the statesmen of the late
eighteenth century and the nineteenth actually found themselves—namely, at the head of political systems of increasing
diversity, a diversity that was fueled by a growing ethnic
nationalism, in a world in which war was not the social
and physical calamity that it is today—did the balance-of-
power system serve the world so ill? Did it deserve the op-
probrium that liberal idealists from Cobden to Woodrow
Wilson heaped upon it? Did they not hold what Kenneth
Thompson has called "a popular and widely held view . . .
that statesmen have a choice between policies based upon
the balance of power and more desirable policies based on
morality and justice"? [3]

It is when we look at the means of the upholders of the

[3] In "Toynbee and the Theory of International Politics," *Political Science
Quarterly,* September 1956.

classical system that we at last see the problems of operating
its counterpart today. Some give us little trouble; for instance, the importance of diplomacy and intelligence or,
as Francis Bacon put it, that "princes do keep due sentinel";
or the concept of alliances against powers that are getting
overbearing. "By alliances, Sir," said Walpole, "the equipoise of powers is maintained and those claims and appre-
hensions avoided, which arise from the vicissitudes of empire and the fluctuations of perpetual contest." [4] True, we
must consider the inflexibility of modern alliance and coalition as an instrument of equipoise, for some alliances have
probably outlived their function.

Another principle, that of moderation on the part of the
major actors, presents us with less difficulty than it did a
generation ago when we were still coping with the consequences both of immoderate action by the Axis powers
and of the Allied commitment to unconditional surrender.
The moderation of means and objectives is the basis of all
our contemporary thought about limited war and crisis
management. It was the governing principle in Truman's
restraint of MacArthur in Kòrea, of Kennedy's refusal to
exploit his diplomatic victory over Khrushchev after the
Cuban missile crisis, of an earlier phase of Soviet policy on
the subcontinent which enabled Kosygin to make peace
between India and Pakistan at Tashkent, and even of President Johnson's refusal to escalate the Vietnam conflict beyond a certain point. At a different level of policy, that of
technological moderation, it was the basis of Secretary of
Defense McNamara's insistence on maintaining a stable
level of secure and dependable strategic forces rather than

---

[4] Quoted in Edward Gulick, *op. cit.*

exploiting American scientific and productive resources to the full. Much of what was once glorified as the "moderation" of a statesman like Bismarck we might now ascribe to the rules of mutual deterrence, to the search for stability through arms control, but the effect may not be dissimilar.

However, there are certain aspects of the classic system of order that are difficult to apply to our present dilemmas. First of all, there is the problem inherent in a multiple relationship of powerful states of who is the holder of the scales and who is in them, who is holding the shifting balance and who is being shifted. Britain, because she had no territorial aspirations in Europe, thought of herself as the balancing element through most of the eighteenth and nineteenth centuries, but this claim was often rejected by her continental partners. If we look at the relative balance of influence, not necessarily power, in Asia today, who is the guardian of the balance? President Nixon, though rejecting any desire to exploit the hostility between China and the Soviet Union, would not, I think, have visited Peking first if he had not seen himself as in some sense adjusting the balance between that capital and Moscow and thus curbing the pretensions of the Soviet Union. The latter, as I have suggested, appears to be embarked on a policy of exploiting the balance of Western and Chinese interests in Asia and the Third World. Some people in Japan see her, like Britain in the eighteenth and nineteenth centuries, as a powerful offshore island which no longer has territorial aspirations on the nearby continent and can therefore act as the future guardian of the Asian balance, if not in a military sense then in terms of political and economic power. That this question can be an important source of confusion was evident in 1939 when both Chamberlain and Stalin and even to some extent Roosevelt saw their countries as the balancing agent and therefore refused to commit them until too late, until the balance had been overthrown. Here I think the analogy of the mobile in which every part interacts with every other is less dangerous and less misleading than the analogy of a pair of scales.

A second and legitimate criticism of the old system is that it assumed a greater flexibility of action and maneuver on the part of the major actors than in fact they were capable of exercising. A writer like Lord Brougham in the middle of the last century could assert that "all particular interests, prejudices or partialities must be sacrificed to the higher interest . . . of unity against oppression or against measures which appear to place the security of all in jeopardy." But, with the increasing articulateness of public opinion in the democracies and the development of ideological policies in the autocracies, the principle became harder and harder to apply, particularly in the wake of great wars like those of 1870, 1914, and 1939, which left a legacy of national bitterness among states whose interest it might well have been to combine for the sake of international order. As a modern American political scientist, Kenneth Waltz, has put it, "In the history of the modern state system, flexibility of alignment has been conspicuously absent just when in the interest of stability it was most highly desirable." [5] This remains true even though the *Ostpolitik* and its responses, the alignment of China and Pakistan and of India and the Soviet Union, as well as the American decision to withdraw troops from Taiwan, show that the moral or ideological

[5] "The Stability of a Bipolar World," *Daedalus*, Summer 1964.

values of the cold war years, democracy versus communism, nonalignment versus alignment, no longer impose the inflexibility upon the international system that they did fifteen or even ten years ago. But the system is always more turgid, more intractable, than the idealists of balance of power have been prepared to admit, and this rigidity has, if anything, increased down the generations. It might, for instance, make political sense to construct a new alignment of the United States, China, and Japan to counterbalance Soviet power in Asia, but, by the time this would become politically feasible, the conditions which made it desirable might have changed.

Finally, the opponents of the old balance-of-power system have always pointed to the fact that an essential condition of a multiple balance was a readiness to resort to war or intervention to checkmate ambitions that were not amenable to diplomacy. Its proponents were quite candid about that; in the days when military technology was still primitive (that is, until about a hundred years ago) this was not the most damaging charge that could be leveled against it. But, as our fear of war and our distrust of physical intervention have increased, so our skepticism about any pattern of interstate relations which predicates its possibility has increased also. There is, however, some confusion on this point. For one thing, any structure of relationships between strong and autonomous centers of power, or even between strong and weak ones, relies *au fond* on the ability to coerce, whether it be a wholly bipolar structure exercised through extensive alliances and by means of long-range thermonuclear weapons, or a form of collective security as expressed in Chapter VII of the United Nations Charter, or the multipolar relationship of an aggregation of small African states—in other words, any situation that is short of general and complete disarmament of a kind in which military power could never be remobilized.

But the nineteenth century multiple-balance system produced two long periods of peace. Among the principal actors, Britain and France have never been at war since 1815, even though they were in an acute arms race in the mid-nineteenth century, and even though Britons have since fought Frenchmen. Britain, France, and Russia have suffered only two minor and limited armed collisions in the past century and a half, the Crimean War and the anti-Bolshevik interventions of 1919–21. Moreover, the modern bipolar system has had no better record while it has lasted than the multipolar. Quite apart from the conflicts of de-colonization or those caused by the shaky local power balances which the retreating colonial powers left behind them, the Korean war drew into its orbit nearly twenty countries and in any earlier period would have been regarded, by reason of its duration and ferocity, as a major war. Three Arab-Israel wars and four wars between India and her neighbors, which the great powers were unable or unwilling to prevent, and an ongoing conflict in Vietnam of more than fifteen years which for at least five or six years had many of the characteristics of a major war, by no means form a blank entry in the ledger, even though there is no question that the bipolar balance of two superpowers and their allies has prevented war in Europe so far.

But let me make myself quite clear. I am not looking at the system of the past with any sense of nostalgia, but simply trying to discover what its objectives and techniques were, where they are relevant today, and where we must improvise in situations which, whether we like it or not, power in the sense of influence, power as distinct from force, power in its broadest sense, is becoming neither institution-alized nor widely diffused but in effect is aggregating around five major centers in the northern hemisphere.

* * *

To provide sharper focus on this question, I think it useful at this stage to look at the many ways in which the meta-phor "balance of power" has been employed. At best it is no more than an analogy; at worst it is a substitute for thought. In a seminal essay on the subject, the late Martin Wight, a distinguished British scholar in the field of interna-tional relations, drew up a list of nine different ways in which the term has been employed, of which I should like to comment on five.[6]

The oldest and also in a sense the most modern use is that of an *even distribution of power*. It embraces attempts to describe situations in which European or world politics were dominated either by a simple equilibrium between two great agglomerations such as the Valois and the Haps-burgs or through a bipolar relationship like that of the Triple Alliance and the Triple Entente or the postwar So-viet-American relationship, as well as situations like post-1815 Europe in which no power stood head and shoulders above the others. It was thought throughout much of the 1950s that nuclear weapons were going to have this equaliz-ing effect, irrespective of the basis of state power on which they rested, just as in the 1850s men like Cobden and Bright

[6] "The Balance of Power," in *Diplomatic Investigations,* edited by Herbert Butterfield and Martin Wight (London, 1966).

thought free trade would equalize disparities of power. It was presumably in this sense of equalization that the previous Leffingwell lecturer, Lester Pearson, used it when he said in San Francisco in 1955, "The balance of terror has replaced the balance of power." Power in this usage meant primarily strategic power, but the whole notion of equality or parity inevitably becomes increasingly distorted and confusing when other forms of significant power or influence —political, psychological, economic—begin to be generated by states inside or outside the bipolar strategic balance.

A more abstract variant of the concept is the *inherent tendency of international politics to produce an even distribution of power*. Thus Toynbee argued that "the Balance of Power is a system of political dynamics that comes into play whenever a society articulates itself into a number of mutually independent local states." [7] Thus Rousseau: *"Ne pensons pas que cet équilibre si vanté ait été établi par personne, et que personne ait rien fait à dessein de la conserver: on trouve qu'il existe."* [8] It is really an unconscious adaptation to the international political system of biological or ecological principles, and many modern historians have disputed its validity as a principle or as having much contemporary application. But it was on this assumption that many political scientists, American and French in particular, argued ten years ago that widespread nuclear proliferation was inevitable. This has not happened, and, as I shall argue, it is not likely to happen. What we have seen instead is a much more complex distribution of different kinds of state power.

[7] Quoted in Butterfield and Wight, *op. cit.*
[8] *Ibid.*

A second classical meaning, that of the principle of *equal shares for the great powers at the expense of the lesser*, is of contemporary relevance, for it accounts for much of the distrust, some of it only half-articulated, that is felt in the Third World for the evolving pattern of great-power relationships. One of the standard devices of the international system has been for the major powers to make adjustments among themselves by dividing or trading some third area in which they had a primary but not vital interest: the obliteration of Poland in the 1790s, the battle for the Chinese concessions in the 1890s, the scramble for Africa, the Anglo-French carve-up of the Ottoman Empire in the 1920s, Poland again in the 1940s, the Korean Peninsula in the 1950s. If this has happened in the past in the name of the stability of a multiple great-power balance, why should it not happen again in Southeast Asia in the 1970s or 1980s? Has it already happened with Taiwan? I shall try later to suggest some of the new defenses which the small have acquired against the big, but it is a tendency and an anxiety of which we in the industrial world must not lose sight unless we wish to give some impetus to a phrase and a new concept of balance that is at present meaningless, namely, "the North-South balance."

A third meaning to which I have already referred is that of *holding a special role in maintaining an equilibrium* or even distribution of power. "There she sat," as Camden wrote of Queen Elizabeth I, "as an heroical princess and umpire between the Spaniards, the French and the Estates." The British have less often played this role than they have thought—for brief periods in the eighteenth century, for about twenty years in the mid-nineteenth. Catherine the

Great probably held the balance between Britain and the anti-British coalition in Western Europe during the American War of Independence; for a while the Iroquois held it between the British and French in North America. Bismarck saw himself as, and indeed was, the arbiter of the European balance in the 1870s. The United States held it between the Allied and the Central Powers from 1914 to 1917. Perhaps Chou En-lai thinks he holds it now. It particularly titillates the fancy of powers on the way up or the way down; some Japanese and some Western Europeans now see themselves as the protagonists of equilibrium, as the conciliators between the superpowers if not the arbiters. "France," said President de Gaulle in 1959, "in equipping herself with nuclear weapons will render a service to world equilibrium." [9] And Harold Macmillan said something very similar about British nuclear weapons two years earlier. At the heyday of its influence in the 1950s and before the quarrel with China, Nehru's India saw herself in the role of equilibrist, though in a moral not a physical sense.

The role of the man in the center, upholder of the system, often slides imperceptibly into a fourth meaning: that my side ought to have *a margin of strength* in order to avert the danger of power being unevenly distributed. This was the sense in which Robert McNamara in his many official statements and speeches as Secretary of Defense in the 1960s always used the term "balance of power": a healthy superiority in strategic forces to deal if necessary with the Soviet Union and China, to limit damage to the United States in a nuclear war, together with a general Western parity with the Communist powers in non-nuclear forces. It was by reference to concepts of world order and the

[9] *Ibid.*

balance of power, often called "countervailing power," that the United States became committed to the freedom and stability of an ever expanding group of countries, old and new, allied and nonaligned, while the Soviet Union had a much smaller range of commitments and a different conception of order. It was in the name of resistance to "the obsolete imperialist conception of the balance of power" that the Soviet Union first verbally then physically negated such strategic superiority.

Finally there is the most primitive concept of all, *predominance*. *"Nous tenons la balance de l'Europe,"* wrote Napoleon to the Directory in 1797. *"Nous la ferons pencher comme nous voudrons."* [10] It was this imperial conception of the balance which led him to reject Talleyrand's plea eight years later for French moderation toward Austria and the restoration of the European state system, and to embark upon that attempt to subjugate Europe which led to his eventual downfall.

Perhaps such a conception of the balance of power still lurks in the back rooms of the Kremlin and the Forbidden City. For, unlike the United States, which became in 1947 committed to what was merely a global strategy—containment—not a global ambition, any country that subscribes, however nominally, to Lenin's interpretation of the *Communist Manifesto* must conceive of balance in terms of eventual predominance: the working class over the bourgeoisie, the countryside over the cities.

But it would be wrong to assume that the United States has never interpreted the balance of power, whether *faut de mieux* or deliberately, in this way. That it has had its local application, American preponderance in the Western hemi-

[10] *Ibid.*

sphere, has been accepted for nearly two centuries. "We may hope," wrote Alexander Hamilton in *The Federalist* in 1787, "to become the arbiter of Europe in America, and to be able to incline the balance of European competitions in this part of the world as our interests may dictate. . . . Our situation invites and our interests prompt us to aim at an ascendant in the system of American affairs." [11]

But 180 years later, when the power and responsibility of the United States had expanded beyond recognition while the vitality of other centers and sources of power was still more a matter of speculation than of fact, Americans, some Americans, were talking not of balance but of predominance. McNamara's famous Ann Arbor speech of 1962, though it contained much good sense, also asserted quite flatly the necessity for a position not only of American strategic superiority over the Soviet Union but also of complete strategic hegemony within her own alliance system. In 1967 Zbigniew Brzezinski, then in the State Department, spoke as follows:

> If we look at the last 20 years there has been a shift from a period, first of all, of polycentrism in international affairs, to a period of bipolarity, to what is today a period of U.S. paramountcy. . . . The U.S. today is the only effective global military power in the world. Moreover . . . our way of life is still the most appealing way of life to most of the people on earth. . . . We are the only power with far flung global economic investments, economic involvement and global trade, and there is no parallel to us in the role our science and technology plays throughout the world.[12]

[11] *Ibid.*
[12] *Department of State Bulletin*, July 3, 1967.

His conclusion, however, was that such paramountcy might last no longer than a decade. In a book published in the same year, another distinguished American political scientist asked:

> What are the specific key features that single out the United States as an imperial state planted at the focus of the international system? They are three: one is the tendency for other states to be defined by their relation to the United States; another is the great and growing margin for error in world affairs which guarantees that, barring an act of folly, the United States can do no wrong under the unwritten law of the balance of power; and yet another has been the slow, hesitant and still inconclusive movement toward containment aimed at America's supremacy which was wholly legitimately arrived at and largely beneficently exercised.[13]

Yet, less than a year after these two assertions of American predominance, President Johnson ordered a halt to the bombing in Vietnam, as a consequence of fierce domestic and international opposition to an unsuccessful intervention against a small Asian power.

I offer these quotations in no spirit of mockery, for I could find their counterpart in the history of my own country. Throughout the whole nineteenth century after the Congress of Vienna, and most especially after the debacle of Franco-German relations in 1870, Britain saw herself as having a special predominant role in the balance of power. Because her influence was rarely put to the test, she thought of herself as occupying the position of a fulcrum in the

[13] George Liska, *Imperial America* (Washington Center for Foreign Policy Research, 1967).

multiple balance. "She was a central magnet," as two British historians have phrased it, "and around her clustered patterns of alliances composed of other sovereign states." [14] More than that, she regarded herself as the center of domestic liberty and enlightened overseas rule. It was the Boer War, so like Vietnam in its effect, the difficult application of force at a great distance with increasing domestic controversy about its outcome, that made Britain recognize the limitations of her power and influence and rethink her position in the multiple balance—on the one hand, making common cause with Japan in the Pacific so that she could have more resources available in Europe and, on the other, entering into an entente with France.

Let us turn from these categorizations to consider briefly some American attitudes to different forms of balance. I imagine that in its early years the Council on Foreign Relations must have heard many denunciations of the concept itself, akin to President Wilson's famous description of it as "a thing in which the balance was determined by the sword which was thrown in on one side or the other; a balance which was determined by the unstable equilibrium of competitive interests; a balance which was maintained by jealous watchfulness and an antagonism of interests." [15] But the concept of great-power relations as a mobile rather than a pair of scales is not alien to American thought. One of Wilson's greatest idols, Thomas Jefferson, was particularly clear-headed on this subject. His sympathies varied during

[14] F. S. Northedge and M. J. Grieve, *A Hundred Years of International Relations* (London, 1971).

[15] Speech at Guildhall, London, December 28, 1918, printed in *The Public Papers of Woodrow Wilson,* edited by R. S. Baker and W. E. Dodd (New York, 1927).

the Napoleonic wars, for he detested the way the British used their maritime superiority; but in 1814, during the American war with England and when the French were at the height of their power, he wrote, "It cannot be in our interest that all of Europe should be reduced to a single monarchy." And a year later he wrote, "For my part, I wish that all nations may recover and retain their independence; that those that are overgrown may not advance beyond safe measures of power, that a salutary balance may be ever maintained among nations, and that our peace, commerce, and friendship may be sought and cultivated by all." [16]

Moreover, in his way Wilson himself was an equilibrist, for, as Hans Morgenthau has pointed out, he "went to war to prevent a German hegemony; while during the war and at the peace table he proclaimed as his purpose to put an end to the balance of power, he actually tried to prevent the hegemony of the Allies." [17] Thirty years later, Roosevelt, having tried too late to grasp the balance, in effect threw the sword in on one side with Lend-Lease, well before Pearl Harbor; ten years later, Truman did the same. Similarly in the Pacific, the United States was for forty years, from 1905 to 1945, actively or indirectly concerned to prevent Japan from becoming a hegemonial power in East Asia. But here she was acting as one power among many, a power of increasing strength but not a dominant one. The history of the rise of the United States from greatness to dominance and her return to greatness has not yet been written. When it is, the story of the dominant years and

[16] Quoted in Hans J. Morgenthau, *A New Foreign Polcy for the United States* (New York, 1969).
[17] *Ibid.*

the intellectual notions to which they gave rise may be seen as an aberration from her historical tradition.

So much has been written about Vietnam by Americans— the most self-critical of peoples—that I will not attempt to add much to it. I would simply say that, though I am certain that the inner justification of increasing American involve- ment after 1962 was in terms of a threat to a global balance of power of which the United States regarded herself as the central Western pole, or one end of a pair of scales, this involvement represented a serious confusion between power and force, a subject to which I will return. It also illustrated not only what Denis Brogan has called "the illusion of American omnipotence," but also the illusion of American omniscience. The attempt to apply abstract economic con- cepts like cost-effectiveness to an assessment of the incal- culable risks of war and politics was rather evident in the research institutes and the academic community during the years of American paramountcy.

Though I hope I have made it clear that I am no idealist about a multiple balance of power, I think we can thank our stars that the worst of the Vietnam involvement oc- curred during a period when the international system was becoming effectively polycentric, as was not the case at the time of Korea. Deep as are the scars left in one country by the Vietnam war, if the world had still been wholly bipolar in structure, not only would the Soviet Union and China have felt more disposed to intervene directly, but, if Japan, Western Europe, and the rest of the industrial world had been persuaded to contribute forces, the prospects of dis- engagement without a full-scale war in Asia, and perhaps the world, would have been immeasurably reduced. It may be cold comfort for Americans, but any protagonist of international order must rejoice that, even if we cannot for the time being have an effective universal system of collective security, at least peace is divisible. Every act of force on the part of a major power does not now automatically escalate to global proportions.

Nevertheless, there are good reasons why Americans, and not Americans only, look askance at the prospect of a polycentric world. It is nothing so simple as pique at the loss of a position of paramountcy, or, as Bolingbroke put it in the middle of the eighteenth century, "They who are in the sinking scale do not easily come off from the habitual prejudices of superior wealth, or power, or skill, or courage, nor the confidence these prejudices inspire." [18] For one thing, the American scale is not sinking; rather, other power centers are rising in potential and autonomy. For another, the imagery of scales is, as I have said, misleading.

I think there are two special reasons why Americans look with concern rather than equanimity at the development of other powers which can lift some of the burden of world order off their shoulders. The first is anxiety about the political temper of their own country. To quote George Liska again: "Like another parochial country projected into world empire, Castile, the United States seemed to depend on a sense of ideological mission for the inner strength to effect a drastic transition from isolation to global involvement." [19] Even more than the original European democracies, the United States is an ideological community, constitutionally committed to certain ideals in a sense that even a high-

[18] Quoted in Gulick, *op. cit.,* p. 29.
[19] *Op. cit.,* pp. 23–24.

minded state like modern Sweden is not. You will remember the words of the movie producer in F. Scott Fitzgerald's unfinished novel, *The Last Tycoon,* searching in his mind for the basis for a great American epic, "France was a land, Britain was a people, but America having about it the quality of an idea was harder to utter." Can a society as self-conscious as the United States accept *raison d'état,* which is by no means the same thing as power politics, as its guiding principle, even though political nationalism is now rather fashionable even with the New Left?

Raison d'état is not the most glorious banner that a nation may hoist, and its acceptance is not a difficulty with which Americans alone have grappled. There were many liberal Frenchmen who, remembering the struggles of a generation earlier, loathed the idea of an alliance with Imperial Russia in the 1890s as the containment of Imperial Germany came to seem imperative. There were many Christian Englishmen in the last century who could not understand the solicitousness of various British governments for the independence and survival of the Ottoman Empire, or see why their country should conclude a bilateral treaty with an atheist Asiatic power, Japan, in 1902. In 1950, many Europeans who had suffered five years of occupation and torture were dismayed that the United States should, in the name of the balance of power, insist on finding a formula for the rearmament of Germany. But, in effect, the binding decision to respect the principle of balance was made a quarter of a century ago when the United States opted to contain rather than destroy the Soviet Union, while accepting the diverse consequences of that decision. One can argue that the role of public opinion imposes a severe constraint on the freedom of governments, but historians would point out that it is in many ways more manageable than the pattern of dynastic allegiances which impelled eighteenth century governments to war, often against their better judgment.

The other concern is more modern, namely, whether, in a world where states generate enormous power, when the two superpowers have acquired the ability to destroy each other and each other's allies several times over, stability and safety cannot be preserved unless these powers have a dominant position in the world and no third party can confuse the signals in a crisis. As Kenneth Waltz has put it, "It is to a great extent due to its bipolar structure that the world since the war has enjoyed a stability seldom known where three or more powers have sought to cooperate with each other or have competed for existence." [20] The fact that this view was broadly accepted in Washington accounts for the anomaly that the United States, which for twenty years has urged West European political and economic unification as a form of burden-sharing, has never encouraged the development of European, let alone Japanese, strategic power. And this desire for strategic bipolarity finds its mirror image in Soviet anxiety about the development of Chinese strategic forces. Nevertheless, the plain fact is that a multiple balance of power, economic and political, is the emerging pattern—*on trouve qu'il existe*—even though at the strategic level it may remain primarily bipolar.

[20] "The Stability of a Bipolar World," *op. cit.*

III

Options and Obligations

In *Time* magazine's issue of January 3, 1972, President Nixon was quoted as follows:

> We must remember that the only time in the history of the world that we have had any extended periods of peace is when there has been a balance of power. It is when one nation becomes infinitely more powerful in relation to its potential competitor that the danger of war arises. So I believe in a world in which the United States is powerful. I think it will be a safer world and a better world if we have a strong, healthy United States, Europe, Soviet Union, China, and Japan, each

77

balancing the other, not playing one against the other, an even balance.

It is a curious statement if taken at its face value, for not only is it historically untrue—a pentagonal balance of power produced two periods each of about forty years of peace between the battles of Waterloo and the Marne and hardly existed afterwards. In "the history of the world," which is a very long one, the longest periods of peace have been those of partial or universal empire. In addition, it negates a long-standing American declaratory position against a multiple power balance, symbolized by President Wilson's famous description of it which I have quoted. It abrogates at least a decade in which it was the conventional wisdom in Washington that the United States should be "infinitely more powerful in relation to its potential competitor." And finally it assumes that, as in the eighteenth century, the five powers concerned have broadly the same range of resources at their disposal. This simply is not true today. The Soviet Union and the United States possess an abundance of strategic, military, and economic resources which the other three partners do not. Western Europe, the United States, and Japan are advanced technological powers of a kind which the Soviet Union and China would like to be but are not. Western Europe has still only the characteristics of an enlarged market, and it will take her many years to acquire those of a single actor in world politics. Japan is not a military power in the ordinary sense; and, if she were to become one, it might destroy the very system of balance of which the President speaks.

Before discussing whether the President is talking in

archaic terms or not, I think it important to make a personal effort to assess which levels of power are likely to be most significant in the 1970s. Is strategic power, which since 1945 has been expressed largely in terms of the ownership of nuclear weapons and later in terms of relatively invulnerable long-range means of delivery, going to remain the dominant form and expression of national power, that which differentiates the great from the less great, the secure from the less secure? It is an important question because so much of the best American work on the systemic analysis of international politics, that by Kaplan, Deutsch, Waltz, and Rosecrance, has used the centralization or diffusion of the ownership of nuclear strategic weapons as its touchstone. My instinct would be to doubt it, except that one must, of course, make provision in one's own reflections for some unforeseen crisis which would polarize the world again and provide a graphic reminder of the vast nuclear armories which the Soviet Union and the United States alone possess and which would again preoccupy other governments with strategic and security problems. But that either superpower or even any third power would deliberately return to the diplomacy of brinkmanship seems to me improbable. Indeed the Soviet-American agreements of 1971 and 1972 on the handling of nuclear crises, and accidents, seem to substantiate this view. Thomas Schelling's "balance of prudence" shows signs of becoming the norm at this level of power.

At the same time one can, I think, detect a diminishing confidence on the part of the smaller nuclear powers that their own armories give them either real influence in the world or real security, which is not to say they will dispense

with them, especially as China perceives the Soviet Union
as an active menace to her territorial integrity. There may
well be important shifts in the way in which the two strategic superpowers maintain their posture of mutual deterrence, a gradual replacement of land-based by underwater
missiles of all kinds, for instance. But two factors which are
common to all the nuclear powers, great and not so great,
are concern with the cost of accepting the dictates of technological innovation and a growing readiness to distinguish
between the possible and the desirable. If negotiated arms
control agreements have not provided the decelerating influence on the arms race that I, among others, hoped ten
years ago that they would, the cost of innovation and the
increasing nonmilitary demands upon public resources are
having an analogous effect.

These considerations are also present in the councils of
advanced non-nuclear powers, even though they may still
wish to keep their options open; the Nonproliferation
Treaty, as I said earlier, is still a fragile instrument. But I
detect less concern with the old Nth-power problem than,
say, five years ago. India, a nonsignatory of the treaty, has
effectively come within the strategic orbit of the Soviet
Union; and an Indian nuclear weapons program would
now, I judge, depend on Soviet agreement. Israel was able
to demonstrate five years ago by her martial skill that she
could preserve her security by conventional means alone.
Japan, 80 per cent of whose people live in large cities, is
more doubtful, separated as she is from Omaha and Washington by 10,000 miles of land and water and faced by two
nuclear powers within ten minutes' flying time for a super-
sonic aircraft. But I believe that it would take either a

debacle in Japanese-American confidence or else deliberate American encouragement to make Japan take up this option. In Europe, Germany's steadfast resistance to any proposals for a European nuclear force (an enlarged and integrated version of the British and French national forces) is likely to remain decisive, again unless the United States deliberately encourages a European nuclear force.

To say this is not to challenge the conventional wisdom that nuclear weapons would still probably provide the most potent source of influence in a situation of deteriorating or uncertain security for the major powers and at the crisis points of the world. All I would argue is that it is now a relatively static form of power, which seems not only less likely to be challenged than a decade ago, but also one that will play a less central part in a somewhat more fluid calculation of interests and affiliations than was the case in the cold war years.

But, if this is true of nuclear weapons, whose actual use invokes increasing rather than decreasing horror with the passage of years since Hiroshima, is it less true of military power in general? As Robert Osgood and Robert Tucker have written, force "is the ultimate obstacle to the excess of ambition and power that would otherwise destroy the balance of interests in a cohesive political system." [1] And that we live in a cohesive political system—however differently organized its units are, with whatever different influence upon each other—no one, I think, would dispute. But force in being, the potential use of force, can be a more important form of political influence than force in battle. One of the factors which one cannot discount is that for

[1] *Force, Order and Justice* (Baltimore, 1967).

over twenty-five years Soviet military power has been potential rather than employed, except for brief and decisive
interventions in Budapest and Prague; whereas American
military power, to say nothing of British and French, has
been frequently deployed in action, with all the short-
comings that the conduct of real war shows up. One has
only to travel around the developing world, to the Arab
countries, to Southeast Asia, even to Subsaharan Africa, to
find that there is a mystique—a credibility, if you like—about
Soviet military power, armies as well as navies, and in places
about Chinese military power as well, a mystique which
American military power does not have because its actual
operation has been so widely and so closely scrutinized and
criticized. This situation need not, however, persist.

But how politically significant this distinction is I am not
sure, because the readiness of the big powers to intervene
with military force seems to me to be declining. As Klaus
Knorr has pointed out in his book *On the Uses of Power
in the Nuclear Age,* there has been a steadily increasing
disapproval in the past generation of policies of forceful
intervention. I do not see any American administration
being ready to repeat the Lebanon intervention of 1958 or
even that in the Dominican Republic in 1965 unless it has
the direct mandate of a large number of other states. And
the same inhibitions operate on the other major powers.
The difference in the Soviet handling of the Czech crisis,
the Polish uprising, and the sustained Rumanian defiance
of the Kremlin's leadership is instructive even if it is not
decisive. It is military aid rather than deployed force which
has become the accepted form of intervention in the Third
World, and one of the ways in which the times are out of
joint is that the Soviet Union has an active policy particu-

larly concentrated on the Middle East, India, and North Vietnam; China has a more modest but competitive one; while the American military aid program meets increasing opposition in Congress, and the military sales programs of the European powers are, for the most part, crass commercialism. If one could envisage any concert of the five major power centers—which I cannot for the time being—the arms trade would surely come high on the agenda of their congress.

There is, of course, an area where deployed American military power is still of great significance, namely, Western Europe—not simply because it amplifies what is really a very modest counterpoise to the forces of the Warsaw Pact in Central and Southern Europe but also because of the link that has always been perceived between the American military presence in Europe and the commitment of strategic power in a crisis. We shall have difficulty in maintaining this counterpoise over the next decade as not only American but European military manpower systems evoke diminishing support, especially from the generation that has never known the threat of a major war. I do not think that a negotiation on mutual force reductions has much promise. The defense of Western Europe may have to be radically reorganized on the basis of a mixture of regular and militia forces, while making greater use of some of the new technology which increases local mobility and the efficiency of non-nuclear barrier forces, as well as enhancing the fire power of the individual soldier. In this process of readjustment, it may be countries like Britain and Germany which will have to play the leading parts in concept and in practice as the United States has done in the last twenty years.

To what extent the Asian allies of the United States will

be successful in implementing the substance of the Nixon Doctrine, increasing their local military efficiency as, in effect, the condition of continuing American alliance with them, I think it is too early to judge. I would simply suggest that, if they are successful, they too will expect to have a greater share of influence on the shaping of joint policy in their area. In other words, the Nixon administration seems to me to have deliberately decided to shift the balance of political influence within the alliance systems of which the United States is still the strategic hub.

As with strategic so with ordinary military power, it is rash to make absolute statements. Some foreseen or unforeseen crisis—a flare-up in Yugoslavia which tempts Soviet intervention, a sharp deterioration of Arab-Israel relations into which the two superpowers get drawn, some major debacle in Africa, another Indo-Pakistan conflict, a military collapse in Vietnam before any agreement on the future relationship of North and South has been negotiated, to look no further than the next few years—may create a new emphasis on the significance of military power. All I would say is that it is now becoming a Western interest to minimize the military aspect of power in a sense in which this was not quite true in the 1950s and the 1960s. And I find it difficult to see that it is in China's interest to maximize it. One can argue, however, that this is not the Soviet view. But may not she be making a serious misjudgment about the temper of our times? May not the cumbersome decision-making machinery in Moscow have deduced from Cuba and Vietnam that we were entering a period when military power was the decisive aspect, only to find by the time the ships and the missiles are built that the rules of the game were changing?

If strategic weapons appear to have become a rather static form of power and the exercise of ordinary military power to be hedged about with important limitations, does this make the exercise of political influence, both within the industrial world and in the "open spaces," relatively more significant? What do we mean by political influence? Obviously, in the world as we know it, political influence cannot be wholly divorced from strategic and military potential, and much of the international relations analysis of the last twenty years has centered almost wholly around the exercise or possession of force. But, unlike force, influence seems to have a number of seemingly unrelated facets. When applied to a great power which is also a great civilization, one aspect is clearly the internal dynamism of its society. Does it provide a magnet for those who are trying to modernize or humanize their own societies? Britain had this effect from the day in the early nineteenth century when Pitt asserted that "Britain has saved herself by her exertions and will, as I trust, save Europe by her example" until fifty years later, when Taine vividly exposed the seamy and unwholesome side of her Industrial Revolution. Germany in the latter part of the last century, with her industrial vigor, Bismarck's social legislation, and the strength of her great universities, played a similar role. For a while in the interwar years before the Stalin purges, it looked as though the Soviet Union might play it. Without question, the United States occupied the same position as the magnetic power from the immediate postwar years until problems like race riots, student trouble, crime, the overloading of the legal system, and the evident problems of the cities destroyed —only temporarily I hope—the unique quality of the United States as "the last best hope of man." Perhaps China, if she would let more people look at her achievements more openly and more closely, could use this form of influence effectively, especially with the leaders of the developing world who face problems not dissimilar to those which Peking faced a generation ago.

A second element of political influence is national will, on which so many Teutonic and Anglo-Teutonic theses have been written: not necessarily the will to fight which most governments have in the last instance, but national will as an aspect of determination to change or maintain the external environment of a particular country or the international environment in general. What proportion of its resources is a country prepared to devote to the achievement of its goals, in terms not necessarily of armed forces but of aid and involvement in the destinies of other states? What risks is a government prepared to take? To what extent is it prepared to assume the political consequences of external economic involvement? To what extent are its primary concerns domestic and its elites inward- rather than outward-looking? How much authority does a government command among the young and the energetic? The last is a problem that has concerned democracies not just for a decade but for generations. The year before I went up to Oxford as a student, the Students' Union voted "that this house will not fight for King and country."

Third, how good is its diplomacy? How sensitive to external susceptibilities is its decision-making apparatus? How consistent is its pursuit of its objectives? And, lest anyone should think that I have in mind the well-documented vagaries of American policy over the past ten years, important though they have been in the loss of American influence in the world, let me remind you that in 1966 Prime Minister Harold Wilson told a Labour Party meeting that Britain's frontier was on the Himalayas, and fifteen months later reached the decision in principle to withdraw all British military power from east of Suez. Consistency is an important strand in the exertion of political influence. But diplomacy has an altogether wider meaning, for it now implies an ability to control the activities of one's own nationals whose independent operations, for instance in the multi-national company, may conflict with other national objectives.

But, if political consistency is one strand in the exertion of political influence, so also is the ability of governments to adapt to changing circumstances and to carry their public opinion with them in the process. Thus, whatever criticism a non-American may level at the Asia policy of the United States of the past decade, the Nixon administration cannot be accused of immobilism.

No one can draw up an accurate balance sheet of the relative political power or influence of the major actors on the world stage today. In terms of political and social magnetism, what writers like Lord Acton have called the "moral factor" in diplomacy, the situation has become, and may well remain, that of a zero-sum game in the sense that no one power, society, or capital city is regarded as the central magnet. What the United States may have lost in terms of influence neither the Soviet Union nor China has really gained, nor Europe either, despite the many close ties of its component countries with different parts of the developing world. But it is bleak fact that, in terms of the will to extend control of her external environment and of consistency in its pursuit of this goal, the Soviet Union is gaining ground which the United States and Europe have lost in the Middle East, on the subcontinent, and in parts of Southeast Asia.

There remains the fourth kind of power, economic power, whose external influence is related, though only in part, to the other three. On this I think I will not attempt to expand what I have already said, beyond expressing my fear that we may be entering a period of "power politics"—something quite different from the acceptance of a balance of power—on the economic plane, a preoccupation with the welfare of my side rather than the general verdure of the international landscape. If democratic governments in particular are unable to find the answer to the unfamiliar phenomenon of growing inflation coupled with growing unemployment, some of the dangerous features of the 1930s are likely to arise again.

* * *

Let me turn now to consider briefly, before examining the actual way in which a new balance may operate, the social and political atmosphere which makes it possible for great states to adjust their relationships without excessive friction or recourse to war. I am sure that Thomas Hobbes was right when he said, "For as the nature of foul weather lieth not in a shower or two of rain but in an inclination thereto of many days together, so the nature of war consisteth not in actual fighting but in the known disposition thereto during all the time there is no assurance to the contrary." [2] My own reading of eighteenth- and nineteenth-century history is that the balance-of-power system worked reason-

[2] *Leviathan*, chapter xiii.

ably well as long as the leaders of the various governments were determined that it should, and that it broke down either when a man of imperial ambition—a Napoleon or a Hitler—was thrown up by the social conditions of his own country or when governments began to lose confidence in the intentions of their partners or to acquire overweening confidence in themselves. The atmosphere of the late nineteenth century, for instance, and the beginning of the twentieth illustrate the latter point. The vulgarization of Social Darwinism had made serious inroads into the judgment of otherwise sensible men, so that Theodore Roosevelt could write:

> The twentieth century looms before us big with the fate of many nations. If we stand idly by, if we seek only swollen, slothful ease and ignoble peace, if we shrink from the hard contests where men must win at hazard of their lives and at the risk of all they hold dear, then the bolder and stronger peoples will pass us by, and will win for themselves the domination of the world.[3]

This sort of attitude had its counterpart in German and British thought. In 1910 a member of Parliament attacked the foundation of the Carnegie Endowment for International Peace with "Does Mr. Carnegie really understand human nature and the immutable laws which govern and guide it? Is the grand law 'the selection of the fittest' to give way to the miserable mediocrity of compromise fostered by charity?" Disparities of power began to prey on the minds of officials, and they became increasingly uncertain that they knew what state power was or how to measure it, so that

[3] *The Strenuous Life* (New York, 1899), p. 200.

jointly and separately they had diminishing control over the course of international politics. I sometimes find it ironic that an era which at the level of painting and literature we associate with a profound sense of quiet and order, the world of Monet and Whistler, of Proust, Henry James, and Edith Wharton, should, at the level of international politics, have been one of increasing tension and mutual suspicion. "If the welfare of England requires it, international agreements can go to the devil," said Admiral Fisher at the Hague Conference of 1907.

Today's world seems to me the converse of this. Though there is a great deal of violence in contemporary literature and malaise in contemporary society, the major governments have less anxiety about each other's intentions, are less prone to saber-rattling, than in the cold war decades, even though they may wish to become more independent of each other. Surveillance satellites, for instance, make it unlikely that we need undergo a self-made crisis like that of the "missile gap" in the late 1950s. Now that a dialogue, however fragmentary, has been restored between Washington and Peking, most of the major centers of power have access to each other's minds. In the Western countries a concern with ecological and social problems, in China the growth of technology and industry, in the Soviet Union the endemic weakness of agriculture and stagnation in certain key areas of science cause a certain sense of introversion which may be the late-twentieth-century equivalent of the mid- and late-nineteenth-century concern with the problems of industrialization and social order.

*   *   *

However, I have delayed too long with generalities and the time has come to look at the world as it is. The first question to be tackled is that of distance. In discussing the evolution of the pentagonal structure of power in the world and in comparing it with such structures in the past in Europe, I have tended to write as if they were all contiguous. But Western Europe is separated by half the globe's circumference from East Asia and has few direct strategic or political interests there. Similarly, China has no direct strategic and only limited economic interests in Europe, though she has an ideological concern in preventing the total consolidation of Soviet power and influence in Eastern Europe. Japan has growing economic ties with Western Europe but only a spectator's interest in the development of, say, the *Ostpolitik*. Therefore we cannot discuss the pentagonal structure as if all the elements were equally reactive to developments in every part of the world, as President Nixon appeared to be doing in the remarks which I have quoted at the opening of this chapter. It is possible, though not, to my mind, proved, that the more reasonable attitude of the Soviet Union toward Western Europe is a consequence of her growing concern with Sino-American relations. But we cannot sustain the opposite argument, that the improvement in the Sino-American dialogue is a consequence of developments in Europe. Moreover, technology has not annihilated distance, and it has become progressively more difficult and expensive to apply power at a distance. The pattern of world trade may be more extensive than ever, but the exertion of conventional land and sea power from afar is much more costly in terms of the resources available than it was one or two generations ago. The prolonged and unhappy debate in Britain on the maintenance of a presence east of Suez in areas like the Persian Gulf and the Malay Peninsula where Britain still has direct interests is a case in point.

But, in terms of the interface of the four levels of power, it seems to me more realistic to think in terms of two different foci of international politics, Europe and East Asia, with only the two superpowers actively engaged at all levels of power, even if certain kinds of development in one area may have an indirect bearing on developments in the other. In both areas the key to maintenance of a stable balance of power seems to me what Marshall Shulman has recently described as "access" or the right of interpenetration, the resistance of claims to exclusive spheres of influence.[4] I note with encouragement that recent American official statements have accepted the principle of mutual accessibility in Latin America.

In Europe, we are groping our way toward a new relationship on two and eventually three fronts; among ourselves, toward the Soviet Union, and eventually toward the United States. The first process has started very late in the day because the 1960s were dominated by an argument about the balance of power in Western Europe itself, whether it would be a French-run system or a genuine coalition of equals. What is involved is not merely the enlargement of the Community, which itself is a difficult process, but also the evolution of political institutions which can enable the European governments to speak with similar if not identical voices in their dealings with the rest of the world, which can agree on the priorities among a very hetero-

[4] "What Does Security Mean Today?" *Foreign Affairs,* July 1971.

geneous assortment of external interests—the relicts of four empires and the consequences of a dynamic but quite un-coordinated series of overseas investments. Also involved are, possibly, the creation of a common military system and, certainly, the evolution of institutions that will permit a more economical use of technological and military resources that are barely adequate to the demands on them.

At the level of strategic power, there is no serious question of Europe's playing the role of equilibrist. Not only is there no requirment to counterbalance American strategic pre-dominance as President de Gaulle mistakenly assumed, but it is acknowledged, in Paris nowadays as well as elsewhere, that the security of Western Europe still depends crucially upon the continuing commitment of American strategic power, on the maintenance of the Atlantic Alliance, and that the development of autonomy at the strategic level is not on Europe's agenda for the foreseeable future.

But the problem of maintaining adequate, deployed mili-tary manpower in Europe to make a European crisis man-ageable is going to present us with a difficult set of choices. Should we by some means or other bribe the Americans to stay in Europe at the level of six divisions, twenty-six air squadrons, and a two-carrier fleet? I am not sure that it would be possible even if we decided to, given the domestic constraints on American military manpower and expend-iture. Moreover, a mercenary relationship is not an easy one. Should the active European members of NATO consolidate their relatively successful cooperation in their Eurogroup, or should they invite France to join with them in creating a new European defense community or system as an offshoot of the Economic Community even if nuclear weapons are excluded for the time being? Somewhere in the next few years—not more—the road forks: either the evolution of a less powerful European grouping within an integrated NATO framework or the evolution of a more powerful, more autonomous system under the umbrella only of the collective alliance. It is difficult to believe that the 1970s can pass without a radical reorganization of the structure and strategy of NATO.

These questions are important, for conventional military force continues to be an aspect of balance in Europe, even though the center of the stage may be held in the next year or so by the preparation and staging of a European Conference on Security and Cooperation. It is at the third and fourth levels of political and economic influence that a tripolar or triangular relationship is beginning to assert itself. Valuable as such events as President Nixon's visit to Rumania may have been in establishing the principle of access, indispensable as was the unity of the Allied negotiating position on Berlin, the fact remains that it is the countries of Western Europe themselves which are playing the leading role in creating a new relationship between the two halves of Europe and which will play the leading role in such a conference. Herr Brandt's *Ostpolitik* may be resisted by some of his own countrymen, but he has become the central figure in developing the conception of a Western Europe with interests of its own, "interwoven," to use his own phrase, "with the rights and duties of the two super-powers." We are witnessing in Europe a continuation of bipolarity at the level of strategic power, and the beginnings of a more triangular situation at the levels of political and economic power. Europe's economic and fiscal interests are not identical with those of the United States, though, as I have said, there is a willingness to make some adjustments by reason of the important strategic and political relationship. By and large, the West European countries accept the principle of "access," whether in the sense of accepting the operation and influence of American multinational companies, Japanese competition within their own economies, or a readiness to maintain a dialogue with the Soviet Union. They do this partly because they hope eventually to establish the same principle in their relations, economic and political, with Eastern Europe.

If the development of a sort of tripolar balance of power in Europe, a small continent scarred with centuries of conflict, with very high levels of mobilized force on either side, is going to be a gradual and tentative affair, the evolution of a major power balance in Asia is already occurring more rapidly. The persistence of Sino-Soviet enmity and distrust, the meteoric rise of Japan as an economic power, the relative decline in Japanese-American confidence, the opening of a Sino-American dialogue, the decision on a partial withdrawal of American power from Pacific Asia—all are factors making for a change in the structure of power and relationships in Eastern and Southern Asia.

Before examining how they may or how they should develop, I would like to offer my own view that this is primarily a quadrilateral relationship. If you consult the textbooks, they will tell you that a quadrilateral balance is inherently unstable because it must polarize into either two against two or three against one. But, if you have only four actors, you cannot invent a fifth simply for the sake of symmetry or intellectual orthodoxy. Western Europe, how-

ever rapidly it coheres, will be too preoccupied with its own
internal organization, with the development of relationships
with the Eastern half of its own continent, and with the
protection of important interests nearer home in Africa or
the Middle East to play a significant role in the politics of
Asia—unless, of course, some major catastrophe should
threaten the eclipse of India or Australia, which, by upset-
ting the whole pattern of relationships in the world at large,
would inevitably draw in all powers with any serious military potential. But, short of such a debacle, I think that
Europe will play much the same spectator's role in relation
to Asia that Japan will play in relation to Europe, with the
difference that, in certain circumstances, individual European powers can continue to play a useful but quite limited
role in the process of nation-building in Southeast Asia.

By the same token, I think it unlikely that India will
play a decisive part in the Asia balance. Now that she is a
Soviet ally, her freedom of maneuver may well be re-
stricted. But in any case her ability to project power of any
kind at any distance from her borders is very limited. She
will be much more concerned with the local balance on
the subcontinent; and even in what I now regard as the
unlikely event of her developing nuclear weapons, these
would be for purposes of local deterrence only. Indonesia,
the other potential partner in the Asia balance, has her
hands full with domestic reconstruction for many years to
come. The influence of Pakistan has been vastly reduced.

It may well be asked whether the United States is going
to remain a leading actor in East Asia. I am one of those
who believe that she will—that David Hume's remarks
about the Athenians who, "finding their error in thrusting

themselves into every quarrel, abandoned all attention to foreign affairs" is not applicable to the American position in the Pacific, or indeed elsewhere. Though President Nixon has narrowed the definition of American interests more particularly in Asia than in any other part of the world, a European observer cannot fail to be struck by the long history of American concern with Asia. After all, her own metropolitan territory stretches half way across the Pacific, and an irredentist Japan or an implacably hostile China could threaten not only her interests but her very security. What clearly is disappearing is an American sense of responsibility for order in the whole of non-Communist Asia —the policy that prevailed from about 1952 to 1968—in favor of concentration on certain key countries (like that which she showed on a smaller scale in the 1960s in regard to Africa). But it must, for instance, remain a major American interest to prevent Japan from quitting the Western military and economic system, even though her presence in it presents difficulties. Clearly, there is still a strong sense of obligation to the Philippines and to Australasia. The difference between the past and the future is that there is less public willingness to consider the actual use of American force to maintain an Asia balance, though its potential use may still be an important factor. Consequently, American influence must be exercised more at the level of political influence and economic power.

Let us examine the positions of the other three partners in the Asian balance. The Soviet Union, as I have implied earlier, is a much more confident power than in the past, but in East Asia her motives seem to be dictated as much by fear as by ambition. She is doing what she can to prevent the expansion of Chinese political influence in Southern Asia and around the shores of the Indian Ocean. In an era of increasing Sino-American dialogue, the Soviet Union cannot be certain that she could use nuclear weapons against China with impunity; this is the virtue of a multiple balance. She has large forces deployed along the Chinese border and in Mongolia, but probably the very last contingency she could face is the prolonged exercise of the second level of power, conventional military force, against China at the end of very long lines of communication. This could weaken her position in Eastern and Central Europe disastrously. By the same token, she needs Japanese and American assistance in the development of Siberia, though she has not as yet shown herself ready to pay a political price for it. In sum, though she has reason to fear Japanese or Chinese dominance in East Asia, I think the Soviet Union will be forced to tread rather more delicately there than in other parts of the world. A false step might convince Japan either that she had no alternative to an indefinite security relationship with the United States or that she must rapidly become a full-scale nuclear power, an autonomous actor at every level. It might also make Peking see a greater congruence of interests with both the United States and Japan than with any other powers.

China, on the other hand, enters this quadrilateral relationship with an almost equal skepticism about the credentials of the three other partners. Even though a mixture of fear, sense of historic wrong, ideological contempt, and anxiety about superpower collusion has made her identify Moscow as the prime adversary for the time being, this implies no necessary confidence in Washington or Tokyo.

Even if the Taiwan issue is gradually settled, as long as there are American military installations in Southeast Asia near China's vulnerable southern border, the United States still has some of the qualities of an adversary state. China's distrust of Japan is based not only on jealousy of the economic dynamism of a country which was once a cultural province of China but also on memories of recent aggression. China is not an expansionist state in the territorial sense. Yet she is proud, unused to participation in modern multilateral diplomacy, and revisionist on certain issues. She has, however, a clear sense of her own vulnerability and will play her hand with caution. If she has an external form of power to exert, it is through the example she can set to the countries of the developing world, and it must therefore be in her interest to widen the compass of the Asian balance.

A triangular relationship of this kind would, I think, be reasonably manageable were it not for the power of Japan. For Japan is a very uncertain actor at every level except that of economic power, although here she may well have as much concern in the next twenty years with the social consolidation of her economy as with its growth. There can be no doubt whatever that she will acquire political interests as her dominance of the markets in Asia extends and as her preoccupation with the problem of access to sources of raw materials continues. But I see no reason to assume that Japan must feel an instinctive urge to translate her economic power into military and strategic power, unless she is deliberately encouraged to or is frightened into it by some debacle in the relations of the other three partners.

Here, then, we have a much more fluid balance-of-power situation than in Europe, operated by four partners of uneven strength, interests, and perspectives. If we look some years ahead, it is possible to conceive a number of variations in the combinations of the players: (1) The *Sino-Soviet alliance,* to contain Japanese economic influence in Asia and oust Western influence for good, may revive. This may be possible after Mao's death but seems improbable if one considers the deep and bitter national and ideological rivalries between the two countries, (2) A *Soviet-American understanding* may emerge out of the SALT agreements, to conduct parallel policies of restraint in Asia in order to neutralize the effect of Chinese nuclear weapons and give Japan no incentive for going nuclear. This has two difficulties. The first is that the Soviet Union would not readily accept the United States as a legitmate partner in Asia, as she does in Europe. Second, it would be certain to incur Chinese, then later Japanese, hostility, without necessarily giving the superpowers any greater control over a local crisis. (3) An *American-Japanese-Soviet understanding* to contain Chinese influence may arise. This variation is possibly an attractive option for Japan, for it would ensure a continuing American strategic guarantee while giving her access to Soviet raw materials and the important Soviet consumer market. Such a pattern, however, would not only embitter China for generations but, in creating a rich man's club, would also arouse the hostility of the rest of developing Asia. (4) There could be a *Sino-Japanese entente* in a situation where the United States plays only a muted role in Asian politics. This combination has certain cultural and economic attractions for Japan: the re-uniting of the twin cultures, closer access to certain raw materials, the prospect of jointly exploiting the China Sea for oil. It has been made more conceivable by the modification of Japanese policy on Taiwan after President Nixon's visit to Peking. But it would be very difficult for China to embrace in ideological terms, despite the prospect of keeping Japanese military power to a low level and giving China access to Japanese technology. If given political form, it might well jeopardize the future of the Japanese-American political relationship; and, of course, for the Russians it would represent the resurrection of the "Yellow Peril" in its starkest form. (5) A bilateral *Russo-Japanese entente* could form. This has some degree of probability if strategic competition is stabilized and the Asian balance comes to be governed largely by economic considerations. On the one hand, Japan could accelerate the exploitation of Siberia; on the other, the consumer market of European Russia is ripe for the kind of products which the Japanese produce so well and so cheaply. But I think it would be a consquence rather than a cause of the change in relationships in Asia. If the United States and Western Europe turn increasingly hostile to Japanese commercial penetration, it is a possibility that must be taken seriously though; if Japan tries to play the role of balancing agent and gives a political context to such an understanding, it will forebode such a decisive shift in the balance of power in favor of the Soviet Union as probably to lead to a modification of European and American tariff and economic policies.

In addition there are a number of other combinations which I find harder to envisage—for instance: (1) a Sino-American understanding at the expense of the Soviet-American and American-Japanese relationships; (2) an American-Japanese-Chinese understanding if Soviet policy passes from the ambitious to the hegemonial, though clearly some Americans do regard this as a possibility; (3) a Sino-American-Soviet entente to contain Japan, which is conceivable only if one believes that Japan is going to acquire not only all the power but also all the ambitions of a super-state in Asia; (4) a Japanese-Chinese-Soviet alliance against the United States, which is not very likely; (5) a four-cornered relationship in which the American-Japanese alliance breaks down but is succeeded by no fresh under-standings between either the United States or Japan and the mainland powers. The last is conceivable but not desir-able, because, if European history has any lesson to teach, it is that a mutually hostile relationship of this kind tends to be balanced at the expense of smaller and weaker powers, a balance of compensation rather than compromise of a kind we have seen before. Fear of this kind of situation is well expressed by a Korean, Pyong Choon Ham: "Ideally Rus-sia would find it most advantageous if America, Japan, and Communist China—all three—checked and balanced each other, rather furiously, affording her the greatest room for manoeuver."[5]

To construct such combinations is a useful intellectual exercise, but it would be a mistake to assume that Asian politics will consist of a continuous series of choices. To do so would belie the facts, as we know them, about modern international politics where swift alignments and realign-ments are not possible as they may have been in earlier multiple balances; choices once made cannot readily be unmade. There are however, other devices than the formal

[5] "Korea and the Asian Power Balance," *Foreign Affairs,* January 1972, p. 343.

alliance: the entente, the implicit or explicit understanding.

What one can envisage is a more elastic system of great-power interaction in Asia in which the relationships of the major actors are not necessarily identical at the four different levels of power; a system in which, for instance, the Soviet Union and the United States maintain their current concern for the stability and safety of the over-all strategic balance; in which China and the United States have a certain level of political relationship, one of reasonable diplomatic intercourse and adjustment, without attempting to hedge in the Soviet Union by the appearance of a more intimate or more collusive bond; in which Japan is neither frightened nor encouraged into an active military, let alone strategic, role in Asia. Though I argued earlier that the politics of the 1970s is not as likely to be dominated by the fear of nuclear diffusion as was feared, the one development, it seems to me, which would impose a dangerous rigidity on the politics of East Asia would be the development of Japanese nuclear weapons. The United States would become dubious about the risks involved in her Asian commitments, China would withdraw again into her shell, the Soviet Union would feel menaced by three powers and would behave either with truculence or with uncertainty. Japan herself would lose much of the influence and respect she is slowly regaining in the small Asian states.

The desirable balance in Asia, therefore, seems to me one in which the status quo is maintained at the strategic level, namely, a continuing Japanese-American security relationship, while greater fluidity in relations between the four major actors at the political and economic levels is accepted.

But such an outcome has two very important concomitants. First, there must be a reasonable amount of communication among all four major actors. The line between Peking and Washington is gradually getting cleared; that between Tokyo and Peking must now be built. For a stable relationship to exist, it is also a Western interest that as high a level of confidence as is possible be restored between Peking and Moscow. The other condition may take even longer to establish; it is nothing less than the recognition by all four capitals of the principle of mutual access in third areas—on the one hand, acceptance of the fact that, in the rest of Asia and indeed the developing world in general, the various powers have acquired certain areas of primary interest, dictated by economic or historical affiliations but, on the other, acknowledgment that this endows none with the right to a hegemonial sphere of influence. The United States may legitimately argue that she has a primary interest in, say, the Philippines and Australasia; the Soviet Union, in India; China, in the Asian Balkan states immediately south of her; Japan, in Indonesia; the European countries, in Malaysia and Singapore. But the difference between primary and exclusive interests must be accepted; all parties must be open to the political, ideological, or economic penetration of the others; the state that claims an exclusive relationship with another country destroys the balance.

To quote that wise observer of the Asian scene, Soedjatmoko, until recently the Indonesian Ambassador in Washington:

In order to make possible a low, non-military, non-political involvement on the part of the major powers while enabling them to play a supporting role in the economic development and modernization of the Southeast Asian nations, there should be at least an implicit agreement among all the major powers to proceed in their relations in Southeast Asia at a low level of intensity and specificity. Such an implicit consensus should be based on a realization that over-involvement of one major power is bound to lead to escalation by others without assurance that the political objectives of such over-involvement would be attained.[6]

I find this sound advice even though it may have certain unpalatable consequences for the United States, such as the quiet demise of SEATO, and, of course, at some point a total military withdrawal from Vietnam.

* * *

I think it will be observed that in the course of these discursive remarks we have moved from any concept of balance as one of crude countervailing power to a philosophy of multiple coexistence. As I have tried to point out, one main rationale and function of a multiple balance in the past has been to preserve the autonomy of its members, while in the process minimizing the risks and scale of war for the reason that the destruction or crippling of one or more of its members destroys the system. The importance of this question of autonomy can hardly be overstressed in looking at Asia, where what are, in fact, four different civilizations meet in the area of the China Sea. But it also has relevance to the European balance as well; Europeans are not Americans, and their civilization is different though the two are closely linked. The autonomous state or civilization has a great deal of vitality, and we are more likely to live in relative tran-

[6] *Survival,* January–February 1972, p. 37.

quility if we respect this differentiation while opposing the temptations of universality for our own values or the claims of other polities.

It may be felt that I have concentrated too much on the relationships of the major power centers and have ignored the other hundred-odd sovereign states in our contemporary world. Not only do some of them, notably those at the interface of so-called great foci of interest like Korea or Yugoslavia or the newly truncated Pakistan, fear that they will be the victims of some great-power agreement over their heads, that they will be the Polands or Taiwans of the future, but many of them are, or will be, also tempted to exploit the multiple balance.

Both aspects seem to me to give a new importance to the United Nations and its agencies. It has proved of limited value as an instrument of collective security, largely because it borrowed from the League of Nations (which in turn had unconsciously adapted it from the Congress of Vienna) the assumption that a concert of the great powers was feasible in an age when the meaning of power, the strength of those who wielded it, and the whole structure of the international system were changing rapidly. And even the *ad hoc* improvisation of U.N. peace-keeping is largely in abeyance because the concept has not yet been adjusted to the existence of a world of more than two great powers. Very possibly the next decade or so may see a regeneration of the United Nations with China a member of the Security Council and with the two Germanys in the Assembly. I, for one, wholeheartedly favor a permanent seat for Japan to be brought about by the reduction of the West European seats from two to one as the Community acquires political validity.

I share, however, Castlereagh's doubts about the legitimacy and durability of the idea of a concert of great powers as the primary means of keeping order everywhere in the world. I see the contemporary value of the United Nations in rather different terms: first, as a permanent seat of contact between the new partners in the two great multiple balances of the world; second, as an arena where the smaller powers can hoist danger signals if they feel themselves the victims of the kind of great-power pressure which I have suggested is no longer legitimate in a multiple balance; third, as a means by which they can drag as many resources as possible out of the developed world to accelerate their own development and mitigate the appalling problems which they face. In addition, of course, the smaller powers are, as in an ecological balance, acquiring new forms of coherence, new means of underpinning their own national identities by local combinations: ASEAN, LAFTA, OAU, and some of the local groupings within the U.N. Economic Commission for Africa.

In the last two generations we have forgotten, and by "we" I mean Moscow and Peking as much as Washington or Brussels or Tokyo, the means or the conditions for maintaining a multiple balance. One is the importance of diplomacy, which is both more onerous and more significant than in the simple world of the cold war. It involves a sensitive concern for the interests both of adversaries and of friends, a skilled knowledge of the sensibilities of other governments and other cultures. It is a skill which is as important in embassies abroad as in the national capital and which in my view cannot be sustained by *ad hoc* teams of political advisers, however brilliant, but only by a permanent corps of experienced professionals. Occasional summit meetings, bilateral or multilateral, are no substitute for abiding by Bacon's maxim that "princes do keep due sentinel." Two American political scientists for whom I have great regard laid down the following dictum some years ago: "As the number of independent actors in the system increases, the share of its attention that any nation can devote to any other must of necessity decrease." [7] I think that this is simply not true as a dictum, though it is true that it takes a very much more professional system of assessment and decision-making than many major capitals now have in order to operate a multiple system. A second condition is consistency in policy so that over a long period of time governments have a clear sense of each other's central interests. And allied to this is the question of domestic stability and a bipartisan perspective on foreign policy, which is by no means to suggest that domestic controversy or electoral argument on the subject must be excluded. Finally, there is the necessity of restraint or moderation in our demands upon the international system, economic as well as political. For instance, a trade war among the democracies would undermine the prospect of balance at other levels and among all partners.

Lest it be thought that these remarks are directed particularly at the United States, let me say that they present an equal challenge to all the major power centers. The Soviet Union seems at this moment to have some of the ambitions of an old-fashioned imperial European power and by its emphasis on exclusive spheres of influence undermines the principle of accessibility or interpenetration which

[7] Karl Deutsch and David Singer, "Multipolar Systems and International Stability," *World Politics,* 1964.

I believe is central to the notion of balance.[8] The Soviet Union, therefore, may have the most to learn about the new rules of the great game. Japan has yet to learn the lesson of economic moderation and restraint as an essential constituent of her autonomy. Western Europe has still to create the very decision-making machinery which is necessary to identify its essential interests.

* * *

To conclude, I feel that I have been able to offer only the most preliminary analysis of the new multiple, central balance or balances of power, whose reality, though discussed in theoretical or predictive terms by academics for some time past, has only become fully manifest in the past year or so. The history of earlier balances of power may offer little practical guidance as to how the two great multiple balances of the next decade will operate. For one thing, we have no experience of the application of the principles of a multiple balance to a situation in which the major actors can generate so much power that explicit agreements, especially on the strategic and economic planes, are required, even between adversary partners, to keep it under control. Indeed, we have no experience of a four-plane multistate

[8] Since these words were drafted the Soviet Union seems, under the eleventh heading of the Statement of Basic Principles of U.S.-Soviet Relations, dated May 26, 1972, which was signed by Nixon and Brezhnev, to have disavowed the concept of exclusive spheres of influence. The President emphasized this point in his report to Congress on June 1: "They [the principals] disavow any intention to create spheres of influence." But the test of whether this is more than words will be the Soviet attitude to Western pressure for greater freedom of movement and accessibility between the two halves of Europe in the forthcoming European Conference on Security and Cooperation.

balance, with an uneven distribution of power among the different actors on the different planes of the kind which I here tried to analyze; and we can only make general, not specific, assessments of how differences in the distribution of power at one level are likely to affect its distribution on another. For another, we have no historical experience of the operation of a multiple balance in a world of 130 sovereign states—there were some 45 in the pre-1914 international system—or one in which the autonomy of the major actors is to varying degrees circumscribed by participation in a network of international organizations. Above all, the history of the modern states system over the three and a quarter centuries since the Peace of Westphalia provides no certain answer to the question of whether the successful operation of a multiple power balance has been a cause or a consequence of a general desire for peace.

All that I have said could be summed up in the simple proposition that we live by our own choice, and to a significant extent an American choice, in a plural world in which the important sources of power have been neither abolished, institutionalized, nor diffused, but have tended to aggregate in uneven ways around a small number of great states. The modern international system springs primarily from the minds and the experience of Western man and Western civilization, with the need to wrestle with analogous situations in the past. The intellectual challenge of the next decade is both to use and to modify this great historical tradition, flawed but also enriched by sporadic failure, to provide an interim accommodation with other civilizations and ideologies in an intractable social order which limits our ambitions but must not suspend our efforts. Yet it would be a sorry world and one that risked alienating not only the lesser powers but our own younger generation as well if they were asked to believe that a balance of power is the highest political achievement of which the new great powers are capable.

Index

COUNCIL ON FOREIGN RELATIONS

Officers and Directors

David Rockefeller, *Chairman of the Board*
Grayson Kirk, *Vice-chairman*
Bayless Manning, *President*
Frank Altschul, *Secretary*
Gabriel Hauge, *Treasurer*

W. Michael Blumenthal

Zbigniew Brzezinski

William P. Bundy

William A. M. Burden

Douglas Dillon

Hedley Donovan

Elizabeth Drew

George S. Franklin, Jr.

Caryl P. Haskins

Joseph E. Johnson

Henry R. Labouisse

Bill D. Moyers

Alfred C. Neal

James A. Perkins

Lucian W. Pye

Robert V. Roosa

Marshall D. Shulman

Cyrus Vance

Martha R. Wallace

Paul C. Warnke

Carrol L. Wilson

Recent Publications

FOREIGN AFFAIRS (quarterly), edited by Hamilton Fish Armstrong.

THE UNITED STATES IN WORLD AFFAIRS (annual), by Richard P. Stebbins and William P. Lineberry.

DOCUMENTS ON AMERICAN FOREIGN RELATIONS (annual), by Richard P. Stebbins with the assistance of Elaine P. Adam.

FIFTY YEARS OF FOREIGN AFFAIRS, edited by Hamilton Fish Armstrong (1972).

THE FOREIGN AFFAIRS 50-YEAR BIBLIOGRAPHY: New Evaluations of Significant Books on International Relations, 1920–1970, edited by Byron Dexter (1972).

THE WEST AND THE MIDDLE EAST, by John C. Campbell and Helen Caruso (1972).

THE UNITED STATES AND THE INDUSTRIAL WORLD: American Foreign Economic Policy in the 1970s, by William Diebold, Jr. (1972).

THE WORLD THIS YEAR: 1972 Supplement to the Political Handbook, edited by Richard P. Stebbins and Alba Amoia (1972).

AMERICAN AID FOR DEVELOPMENT, by Paul C. Clark (1972).

THE CARIBBEAN COMMUNITY: Changing Societies and U.S. Policy, by Robert D. Crassweller (1972).

INDIA, PAKISTAN, AND THE GREAT POWERS, by William J. Barnds (1972).

CONGRESS, THE EXECUTIVE, AND FOREIGN POLICY, by Francis O. Wilcox (1971).

THE REALITY OF FOREIGN AID, by Willard L. Thorp (1971).

POLITICAL HANDBOOK AND ATLAS OF THE WORLD, 1970, edited by Richard P. Stebbins and Alba Amoia (1970).

JAPAN IN POSTWAR ASIA, by Lawrence Olson (1970).

THE CRISIS OF DEVELOPMENT, by Lester B. Pearson (1970).

THE GREAT POWERS AND AFRICA, by Waldemar A. Nielsen (1969).

A NEW FOREIGN POLICY FOR THE UNITED STATES, by Hans J. Morgenthau (1969).

MIDDLE EAST POLITICS: THE MILITARY DIMENSION, by J. C. Hurewitz (1969).

THE ECONOMICS OF INTERDEPENDENCE: Economic Policy in the Atlantic Community, by Richard N. Cooper (1968).

HOW NATIONS BEHAVE: Law and Foreign Policy, by Louis Henkin (1968).

THE INSECURITY OF NATIONS, by Charles W. Yost (1968).

PROSPECTS FOR SOVIET SOCIETY, edited by Allen Kassof (1968).

THE AMERICAN APPROACH TO THE ARAB WORLD, by John S. Badeau (1968).

U.S. POLICY AND THE SECURITY OF ASIA, by Fred Greene (1968).

NEGOTIATING WITH THE CHINESE COMMUNISTS: The U.S. Experience, by Kenneth T. Young (1968).

FROM ATLANTIC TO PACIFIC: A New Interocean Canal, by Immanuel J. Klette (1967).

TITO'S SEPARATE ROAD: America and Yugoslavia in World Politics, by John C. Campbell (1967).

U.S. TRADE POLICY: New Legislation for the Next Round, by John W. Evans (1967).

TRADE LIBERALIZATION AMONG INDUSTRIAL COUNTRIES: Objectives and Alternatives, by Bela Balassa (1967).

THE CHINESE PEOPLE'S LIBERATION ARMY, by Brig. Gen. Samuel B. Griffith II U.S.M.C. (ret.) (1967).

THE ARTILLERY OF THE PRESS: Its Influence on American Foreign Policy, by James Reston (1967).

TRADE, AID AND DEVELOPMENT: The Rich and Poor Nations, by John Pincus (1967).

BETWEEN TWO WORLDS: Policy, Press and Public Opinion on Asian-American Relations, by John Hohenberg (1967).

THE CONFLICTED RELATIONSHIP: The West and the Transformation of Asia, Africa and Latin America, by Theodor Geiger (1966).

THE ATLANTIC IDEA AND ITS EUROPEAN RIVALS, by H. van B. Cleveland (1966).

EUROPEAN UNIFICATION IN THE SIXTIES: From the Veto to the Crisis, by Miriam Camps (1966).

THE UNITED STATES AND CHINA IN WORLD AFFAIRS, by Robert Blum, edited by A. Doak Barnett (1966).

THE FUTURE OF THE OVERSEAS CHINESE IN SOUTHEAST ASIA, by Lea A. Williams (1966).

ATLANTIC AGRICULTURAL UNITY: Is It Possible? by John O. Coppock (1966).

TEST BAN AND DISARMAMENT: The Path of Negotiation, by Arthur H. Dean (1966).

COMMUNIST CHINA'S ECONOMIC GROWTH AND FOREIGN TRADE, by Alexander Eckstein (1966).

POLICIES TOWARD CHINA: Views from Six Continents, edited by A. M. Halpern (1966).

THE AMERICAN PEOPLE AND CHINA, by A. T. Steele (1966).

INTERNATIONAL POLITICAL COMMUNICATION, by W. Phillips Davison (1965).

ALTERNATIVE TO PARTITION: For a Broader Conception of America's Role in Europe, by Zbigniew Brzezinski (1965).

THE TROUBLED PARTNERSHIP: A Re-appraisal of the Atlantic Alliance, by Henry A. Kissinger (1965).